Curing THE INCURABLE

How to Receive Healing in Hopeless Situations

JACK COE

CURING THE INCURABLE: *How to Receive Healing in Hopeless Situations*

ISBN: 0-924748-52-4
UPC: 88571300022-2

Printed in the United States of America
Originally published by Jack Coe.
Revised Edition © 2005 by Jack Coe Ministries.

Milestones International Publishers
4410 University Dr., Ste. 113
Huntsville, AL 35816
(256) 536-9402, ext. 234; Fax: (256) 536-4530
www.milestonesintl.com

1 2 3 4 5 6 7 8 9 10 11 / 10 09 08 07 06 05

Endorsements

━━━

Having been one who studied the men of God whom God greatly used in the past to bring salvation and deliverance to the masses, it was only a matter of time before I came across the ministry of Jack Coe, Sr. After listening to his teachings on tape, watching videos of his ministry, and reading others' materials on him, it was obvious to me that Jack Coe had great boldness in the Gospel and the same spirit of faith as did the early disciples of Christ. Signs, wonders, and miracles followed his ministry. Reading his materials will greatly inspire and energize your faith.

Reverend Ted Rouse

Faith's Creation Christian Fellowship

4400 Mayfair Rd

Milwaukee, WI 53225

As a child I heard about the ministries of the great healing trailblazers and revivalists. Jack Coe's name was always at the top of the list. His faith epitomizes the strength and power of God. He believed God for the most absurd healings ever. This book chronicles many of those miracles.

Dr. Kervin J. Smith

Author, *Living Single: The Different Faces of Singleness*

President, Kervin Smith Ministries

Is there anything too hard for God? There are some things that man's power is unable to perform. However, with God all things are possible. God can strategically create doors where none ever existed. He can create something out of nothing. In short, God is a God of miracles. If you believe that God still works miracles, *Curing the Incurable* will whet your appetite for a deeper union with the Divine. If you still need convincing on this miracle issue, after you've read this work you will never second-guess miracles again.

Bishop LeRoy Bailey, Jr.
Senior Pastor, The First Cathedral
Author, *A Solid Foundation: Building Your Life From the Ground Up*
Presiding Prelate, Churches Connected and Covered in Covenant

For more than ten years I have conducted healing and miracle campaigns across America. In that time I've witnessed nearly every kind of disease healed miraculously by the power of God. Until now, I really cannot explain how God does what He does. I just know that it happens. *Curing the Incurable* is a living testament that has lasted for nearly half a century and that continues to herald the truth: Jesus Christ is Healer to the glory of God. Essential reading for every REAL believer!

Aaron D. Lewis
Author, *Keys to Unlocking Your Destiny, Healing for the 21st Century*, and *The Total Package: Keys to Acquiring Wealth and Walking in Divine Health*

Contents

Foreword

So many of God's people are bound up with spirits of infirmity...so many sick and afflicted...so many dying of disease. This is not what God intended for His children. Jesus taught us in Matthew 15:26 that healing and deliverance were "the children's bread."

One of the reasons so many continue to suffer is, simply, the lack of teaching. So many who approach God for deliverance are lacking important foundations that would lead them to healing. They remain sick and frustrated because they know God wants them well but don't know how to obtain their healing.

I was delighted to become reacquainted with Jack Coe's book, *Curing the Incurable*. For years I have presented his taped message on the topic, but it has been quite a while since I've actually read the book.

As I read through the teachings of this great general of faith, my heart was stirred with the truths he had learned in his years of preaching and demonstrating the Gospel. He covers much about the proper heart attitudes and preparation of spirit that lead us to healing and deliverance. Many of these truths are left out of other books on the subject.

One of the gifts Jesus gave to the church is the gift of the evangelist, according to Ephesians 4:11. Along with the rest of the fivefold ministry, the evangelist's insight and wisdom were given for the equipping of saints for ministry and for the edifying of the body (verse 12).

Evangelist Jack Coe was a great gift to the church of Jesus Christ. He learned much through his study of the Word and through his exercise of the gift of faith, the gifts of healing, and the working of miracles.

I believe every young minister reading this book will be better equipped to preach the Word with signs follow-ing, and I believe any sick person reading this book will have a new dimension of faith come alive in his or her spirit. Truly the sick will be made whole through reading and receiving the truth of these pages.

I personally commend Evangelist Jack Coe, Jr., for taking up the commission to republish his father's book. Its contents are needed greatly today. More importantly, I am thankful that he is preaching the Gospel of power with clarity and integrity today. The truth of God will always endure to each generation.

When you are finished reading this book, be sure to share it with someone who needs a miracle. I know it will be a great blessing to them.

—Evangelist R.W. Schambach

Foreword

╬═══╬

Over the past century hungry souls have searched out the "healing classics" of our time, expecting to receive from them a new standard in Christ-centered healing. Their search led them to the discoveries of great works such as F.F. Bosworth's *Christ the Healer*, Andrew Murray's *Divine Healing*, and A.B. Simpson's *The Gospel of Healing*. The book *Healing the Sick* by T.L. Osborn was yet another classic that has helped to bring life to millions. Maria Woodworth Etter, in her *Diary of Signs and Wonders*, recorded some of the most amazing supernatural healings and miracles ever witnessed during her time.

At the break of the century, John Alexander Dowie circulated his *Leaves of Healing* periodical. It became not only a standard of healing and the methods of healing for the parishioners at his 4,000-seat church Shiloh Tabernacle in Zion, Illinois, but also the catalyst that sparked revival and renewal around the world. In more recent times Oral Roberts, whose name has become somewhat of a household item, is well known for his miracle tent healing crusades and the university that bears his name. His book, simply entitled *The Miracle Book*, has been distributed to millions of people all over the world who desired to have a clearer understanding of how God's miracle power can be made available to them.

World-famous faith healer Kathryn Kuhlman followed in the same tradition as Roberts with her testimonial styled best-seller *I Believe In Miracles*, which chronicled the stories of people who were positively impacted and ultimately healed through her ministry. Several million Catholic Christians received a clearer understanding of the ministry of healing through the work of Rev. Francis MacNutt, who wrote a stellar work simply entitled, *Healing*. These men and women are just a few of the many people whom God inspired with pen to write works that have not only become treasured classics but also have brought healing to the lives of innumerable people.

Added to this list of great classics, both older and new, is a book that my father, the late great Jack Coe, Sr., wrote many years ago called *Curing the Incurable*. During the 1930's and 40's in America, medical technology was nowhere as far advanced as it is today in the 2000's. People died from many diseases they contracted that today have proven cures and therapies. The insurance industry was not as savvy then as it is now. The concept of Health Maintenance Organizations, better known as HMO's, was not even explored. Times were very different.

Although there were a fair share of skeptics and religious people then, overall, people had healthy respect for God and things that were considered to be sacred. Today, it is rare to find anyone who has dogged convictions about anything that pertains to God, His power, His nature, or even His purpose. This confusion has caused cynicism, doubt, and disbelief to rise concerning health and healing.

Talk shows such as Oprah Winfrey's and news magazine shows such as *60 Minutes* and *48 Hours* recently aired shows that document how several medical doctors here in America are responsible for accidentally killing more than 365 people each day. That number represents the equivalent to a jumbo jet plane crashing every day of the year. These figures are quite shocking and disturbing.

I'll be the first to admit that doctors do have a place within society and have the ability to help many sick people. However, doctors are humans and are subject to error every now and then. And because of that, they at times make judgments that are unfounded and often lethal. Their human frailty should not cause anyone to become paranoid about doctors but rather should cause them to become more eager to seek out the greatest physician ever known, the Lord Jesus Christ. Only Jesus has consistently proven by example and through demonstration that He can heal all disease and sickness. It is Jesus Christ who was the impetus for the creation of this work, convincing my father many years ago that there is absolutely no such thing as an incurable disease.

There are many diseases in the earth for which medical doctors and researchers do not know the cure. That does not say very much. Just because one or more people have not discovered the cure for a particular disease does not mean that the cure does not exist. Just because there are many people within this world who have not discovered the Messiah does not mean that the Messiah does not exist. It simply means that they lack knowledge. And for that reason, we are destroyed.

My people are destroyed for lack of knowledge: because thou hast rejected knowledge, I will also reject thee, that thou shalt be no priest to me: seeing thou hast forgotten the law of thy God, I will also forget thy children (Hosea 4:6).

In its heyday this work sold more than a half million copies. It was intentionally written with a very direct and simple approach to reach the masses with the message of Christ's healing power. I am proud to announce that *Curing the Incurable* has done just that. During the time that this book was in print, literally thousands of letters would flood my dad's office each week with testimonials of how God used this book to heal the writers' bodies from polio, cancerous tumors, high blood pressure, muscular sclerosis, and other so-called incurable diseases.

Often when I preach around the country, someone will inevitably come up to me and mention how my father's ministry and this wonderful work, *Curing the Incurable*, has tremendously blessed his or her life. Because of these repeated occurrences, I felt provoked by the leading of the Holy Spirit to release this special revised edition of this near-forgotten treasure. I believe that this work will once again bring healing to the masses around the world. In a step-by-step approach, you will learn just how to activate and release your faith now to receive God's healing touch in your life.

In its first printing it impacted millions of people around the world. Thanks to new technology, this work will impact literally billions of people around the world. You hold in your hand yet another treasure from the past made relevant to your future. I challenge you to read on and find out how God cured those whom the doctors labeled as incurable. Use this work to receive your healing, then pass it on to someone else who needs healing. Continue to share this work until every person within your circle is completely healed by His power.

Until we meet face to face, be blessed and be healed.

—Jack Coe Jr.
Red Oak, Texas

Chapter One

Five Key Steps to Receiving Your Healing

One of the saddest truths is that there are millions, perhaps even billions, of people in this world today who have never experienced the delivering power of God. There are several reasons for this. One simple reason is that there are still many people who have not heard the Gospel message of Christ's kingdom. Since they have never heard, they cannot believe; they cannot depend on something that they are unfamiliar with.

Although the message of healing has been preached in many remote parts of the world by some of the greatest evangelists and missionaries of our time, still not everyone has had the opportunity to hear what God's Word declares about healing. Around the world, more than 365,000 babies are born every day. These children quickly grow into mature adults. And these adults desperately need to hear a word from God. Even though there are millions who are reached, there are still millions more who have not been reached.

Then there are those who heard the Word but rejected it because of their ignorance. Their ignorance caused them to willingly choose death over life because they refused to embrace knowledge. It may seem like all the people who fit into this category are unbelievers, but that is not true. Many professing believers have accepted Jesus as their Savior yet have not believed on His power to heal them in the here and now.

A large number of these people remain in lifeless churches that neither believe nor teach of Christ's power to heal—and they are tragically dying. As a result, when the Word of God comes to bring healing to them, they refuse it because it does not measure up to their traditional theology. Unfortunately, many people in this category die prematurely, all because they refused to accept what God's Word says concerning divine healing.

Some people become sick and die because they have not heard. Others had the privilege of hearing, but refused what they heard. Still another group exists. These people hear the Word and believe it, but don't know how to release their faith in order to receive their healing from God.

In this chapter I would like to deal with exactly how to receive your healing from God. I am going to cover five areas that I believe are vitally important for you to understand if you are going to receive God's healing power in your life. However, before we begin covering each of these five areas, there are some preliminaries that we need to cover.

First and foremost, you must be sure that you are saved. There is no compromise in this area. You have to know beyond all doubt that you are truly born again, that you are living a righteous lifestyle before God and man.

Secondly, you need to confess your faults to the Lord. Why is this step necessary? Confessing your faults puts God on notice that if there is any potential hindrance in your life—something that may stand in the way of your healing—you are asking Him to take it away.

Thirdly and finally, you have to continue in prayer until you have developed a real and living faith in God.

Just because you don't receive results immediately does not mean you ought to give up or throw in the towel. If there is one thing that you as a believer should recognize, it is the truth that God has made you righteous—and it is the prayers of the righteous that will get the job done. So whatever you do, don't stop praying and don't quit seeking God. Your healing is far closer than you would ever believe. Keep on praying and believing.

Confess your faults one to another, and pray one for another, that ye may be healed. The effectual fervent prayer of a righteous man availeth much (James 5:16).

Step #1: Understand That Faith Comes By Hearing

So then faith cometh by hearing, and hearing by the word of God (Romans 10:17).

Although each of these steps is equal in importance, without mastering this first step the others won't really matter. You must know for sure that faith comes by hearing. In fact, anything that you want faith for, just keep listening. After a while you will have exactly what you have been hearing over time.

I've known brothers and sisters in the church who do nothing but compare stories about their sicknesses, medications, and doctor-prescribed therapies. As a result of hearing all that negative talk, more sicknesses, medications, and doctor-prescribed therapies are exactly what they receive! Whatever you keep on hearing is what will be produced in your life. That is why I choose not to keep company with buzzards but rather with eagles. Buzzards do nothing but fly around all day long being unproductive and talking about what they cannot do. I refuse to associate with that group.

I choose to hang out with eagles. Eagles soar above life's hardships and trying situations. They fly so high that they don't even know what is happening on the lower levels of life. When you choose to develop your faith by only hearing what God's Word says on a matter and not allowing opposing words to counter what God's Word declares, then you will receive what you are believing God to do.

4

You have got to hear what you desire so much that not to receive it is not even an option. You are put in a position where you have to receive because you don't have any other options. All you know to act on is what you have heard. And if what you have heard is the Word of the Lord, then your success is just around the corner. But you have to be very cautious to make sure that what you are hearing on a regular basis measures up to God's Word.

Whatever you hear long enough, will come to pass in your life.

One thing you must do is read your Bible regularly. Reading your Bible develops the God-kind of faith in you. I suggest that, instead of reading your Bible quietly, you do just the opposite: Read it out loud. You need to read your Bible out loud because you need to hear God's Word. It is one thing to read God's Word silently, but it's a whole different thing when you are hearing what you read. When you read aloud, words get into your mind.

In fact, when you hear words spoken aloud, they get into your spirit and your subconscious mind. When they get in there, nothing can erase them. It is *that* kind of hearing that develops and matures your faith in God. Please note that there are two kinds of faith. The first kind of faith is one that God gives you in your hour of need. This kind of faith can be viewed as an emergency or 911 faith. It rises to the occasion of an emergency situation.

But faith that comes by hearing is the kind that has taken time to develop through reading, studying, hearing, and doing what God's Word says to do. This kind of faith is like a marinated faith. If you desire to be wealthy, you will have to hear wealthy talk from wealthy people. You will have to commit to reading, on a daily basis, all the scriptures in the Bible that pertain to wealth. There is no difference with healing. You have to begin reading over and over again every scripture that pertains to healing.

Commit to memory every God-given promise in the Scriptures and begin to recite them every opportunity you get. It's the Word of God that heals. Psalm 107:20 declares, *"He sent his word, and healed them, and delivered them from their destructions."* So the more Word that you get on the inside of you, and the more that you hear it, the sooner your healing will manifest.

When Jesus came off of His 40-day wilderness fast, He was immediately tempted of the devil. The way that Jesus overcame the temptation of Satan was by knowing the Word of God that He had heard before. It was the Word of God that He heard that was used as a defense against Satan when the enemy assaulted Him. Jesus' example makes it clear just how important it is to get the Word of God in our hearing and down into our spirit man so that we have something to act on and use as ammunition against the devil when he attacks us.

Being forty days tempted of the devil. And in those days he did eat nothing: and when they were ended, he afterward hungered. And the devil said unto him, If thou be the Son of God, command this stone that it be made bread. And

Jesus answered him, saying, It is written, That man shall not live by bread alone, but by every word of God (Luke 4:2-4).

This very important passage is directly correlated to your healing. Jesus is trying to convey a message that man does not live by what is natural (bread). His life is directly proportionate to how much Word he receives as a part of his spiritual nutrition plan. Man lives by words. That's exactly what Jesus was saying—man lives by words. No words, no life. Knowledge of His Word will equal a deeper knowledge of life. So the first step toward receiving your healing is to make it your top priority to hear the Word of God concerning healing *consistently*. Your healing is connected to what you hear.

Step #2: Understand That Humility Is Key

By humility and the fear of the LORD are riches, and honour, and life (Proverbs 22:4).

"God resists the proud, but gives grace to the humble" (James 4:6 NKJV). If you humble yourself, God will exalt you and freely give you spiritual gifts of healing. You cannot come to God with an arrogant attitude thinking that you deserve to be healed just because you are so special. Maybe you believe that God should heal you because you have earned high academic achievements. Perhaps you are a high-income earner and believe that

since you earn a six-figure income, you automatically qualify to be healed by Jesus.

Please allow me to inform you that you cannot do anything in the world to qualify you to receive your healing. You are not and never will be so righteous on your own that your righteousness merits healing. Healing is a divine grace and gift of God. You cannot earn a gift; you just receive it as a kind act on the part of the giver. Gifts are not owed to anyone; they are given freely. Only the proud in heart believe that God's gifts can be earned. It is this lack of humility that explains why so many still remain sick.

Submit yourselves therefore to God. Resist the devil, and he will flee from you. Draw nigh to God, and he will draw nigh to you. Cleanse your hands, ye sinners; and purify your hearts, ye double minded. Be afflicted, and mourn, and weep: let your laughter be turned to mourning, and your joy to heaviness. Humble yourselves in the sight of the Lord, and he shall lift you up (James 4:7-10).

The apostle James rightly believed that humility before God will quickly get His attention and approval. You have got to be humble. Humility is not exactly what people think it is. Some people, particularly sinners, believe that humility is a sign of weakness. They believe that humility equals stupidity. That's not biblical. Humility is just the opposite. True humility is a definite sign of strength. It is also a mark of great wisdom on behalf of a person.

True humility says that you possess a teachable spirit and that you are willing to serve in any area God needs you. This kind of humility before God is a necessary step toward receiving your healing. Nothing on earth disgusts God more than a prideful person. Remember this: God has very little mercy on the proud. Pride was the reason Lucifer got kicked out of heaven.

Lucifer was a beautiful angel, a bearer of light. He also was an incredibly gifted musician and singer. One day his abilities and image made him feel that he was indispensable. (Always remember that no one—and I mean no one—is indispensable. There is always someone who can do what you do and do it better.) Lucifer felt so prideful in his abilities that he believed he was better than God and tried to overthrow Him. Listen to his prideful talk as recorded in the book of Isaiah.

> *For thou hast said in thine heart, I will ascend into heaven, I will exalt my throne above the stars of God: I will sit also upon the mount of the congregation, in the sides of the north: I will ascend above the heights of the clouds; I will be like the most High. Yet thou shalt be brought down to hell, to the sides of the pit* (Isaiah 14:13-15).

Lucifer lost his position in heaven as the chief praise and worship leader because of his pride. As I told you before, there is always someone who can do what you are doing and do it better. After Satan lost his position in heaven, guess who God appointed to fill that position? You've guessed correctly—the body of Christ. That's you and me. We now have the easy task of worshipping and praising God and giving Him glory all day long. And as long as you and I stay humble, we will be able to contin-ue in this position. Humility is a big deal to God. It can be the determining factor on whether or not you receive your healing.

Humility can be a determining factor in receiving healing.

During a healing campaign in Philadelphia, Pennsylvania, I prayed for a man who possessed the spirit of humility. His body was completely cancerous. A couple of months prior to his coming to my healing service, he had undergone several major sur-geries in an attempt to get him well again. During the final attempt to cut out all the cancer that had spread, the doctors finally agreed that there was nothing else they could do. They said the cancer was spreading faster than they could actually get rid of it.

They sewed the man back up and sent him home to die. For a short while this man had been subsisting on strained baby food. That night when I prayed for him, the power of Jesus instantly healed him. I even punched him in the stomach in the area where he had been affected the worst and he said he did not feel any pain at all. He began to thank God and glorify God. He made it known that God was a gracious and good God. He said, "I know I don't deserve such mercy, and the only reason I've received my healing is because of His goodness, not mine."

I wish that every person I prayed for had this same attitude. I've asked several people, "Do you believe that God will heal you?" They'll pompously respond, "Oh yes, He will. I've got all the faith in the world. I'm a man or woman of great faith. After all, I've been living for God for more than twenty years." People who talk this way really believe that God will heal them because of their cocky attitude. The truth is that very few people who think and speak like this ever get healed. If they would take the humble position of the centurion soldier, then maybe they would see God's healing hand in their life more frequently.

> *And when Jesus was entered into Capernaum, there came unto him a centurion, beseeching him, and saying, Lord, my servant lieth at home sick of the palsy, grievously tormented. And Jesus saith unto him, I will come and heal him. The centurion answered and said, Lord, I am not worthy that thou shouldest come under my roof: but speak the word only, and my servant shall be healed* (Matthew 8:5-8).

Although this centurion possessed great faith in God, he also possessed great humility before God: *"I am not worthy that thou shouldest come under my roof."* It is this kind of humility coupled with faith that will always produce supernatural results in your life.

I was holding a healing campaign in Chickasha, Oklahoma. A little Pentecostal woman came up in my line a number of times to get prayer for her enlarged tumor. Each time I prayed for her and she did not get healed, she started running off at the mouth blaming the church, the pastor, and of course me as the reasons she could not receive her healing.

She thought that since she was Pentecostal, she automatically qualified to receive healing. She had the wrong attitude and the wrong spirit. She had witnessed a Methodist woman who had come for prayer for hemorrhaging effusions in her body. The power of God instantly healed her. Although this Methodist lady sincerely wanted to be healed, she didn't really know whether or not it would happen for her that evening since she had never spoken in tongues.

In the eyes of judgment-casting Pentecostals, she felt as if she was not as spiritual as they were. So she concluded that if God healed her it would be a high honor, but if He did not she would still love Him just the same. Her humility is what attracted God's healing power. The Pentecostal lady was so upset because the Methodist woman received her healing that she began to voice her complaints. "How did she get healed? She doesn't even speak in tongues, and I do!"

She thought, *The woman does not know about the fullness of God. Her church does not teach the full Gospel like mine does. And, on top of all of that, she does not even have as clear an understanding of the spiritual gifts in*

Corinthians 12 as I do. This woman was full of pride. Later that night, the Pentecostal woman went home and began to cry out to the Lord. "Why? Why, oh why, God, won't You heal me?" She knew within her spirit that she was not exemplifying a humble nature. She repented of her attitude and actions, and immediately God healed her tumors.

If you want to be healed, remember to always walk in humility. God cannot move through the prideful in spirit.

Step #3: Be Careful for Nothing

Be careful for nothing; but in every thing by prayer and supplication with thanksgiving let your requests be made known unto God. And the peace of God, which passeth all understanding, shall keep your hearts and minds through Christ Jesus (Philippians 4:6-7).

Someone recently told me that I should be very careful about publicly sharing the testimonies of those who received their healings in my meeting until each case had been thoroughly examined by the doctors and I'd received a written report from them. They then told me that I should wait at least seven months to make sure that the healing is authentic. I told that person that God's Word says to *"be careful for nothing."* That simply means that I am not going to worry about anything.

When a person comes to the altar in an evangelistic crusade meeting and gives his or her heart to the Lord, no one says that he or she needs to get a written verification of his or her salvation experience. No one tells that person and the evangelist that they must wait at least six months to see whether or not the person will remain saved. We just believe that, according to God's Word, if the person confessed with his or her mouth that Jesus is Lord and believed in his or her heart that God the Father raised Jesus from the dead, then that person is saved.

It is no different with healing. Both salvation and healing are brought about by faith. Hebrews 11:1 says, *"Now faith is the substance of things hoped for, the evidence of things not seen."* Faith is our proof and the material substance of our healing. There are many people who are saved today who will admit that they did not feel the evidence of salvation at the time when God initially saved them. The truth is that it does not matter whether or not you feel saved. We are not saved by our feelings. If we were saved based on feelings, most Christians would be in horrible shape since our feelings have the ability to change as frequently as the wind does.

We are neither saved nor healed by our feelings. Both healing and salvation are products of faith. There are times when it may be days or even weeks before we can actually feel the joy of our salvation or healing. Your joy will only come after you have genuinely accepted the promise of God. You ought to begin praising God and thanking Him for the manifestation of your healing regardless of whether you feel healed or not.

14

Believe me when I tell you that if you start looking for symptoms after you have claimed your healing, the devil will readily and abundantly supply you with as many symptoms as you desire. After you have been healed, it is the devil's job to make you feel sick—even though there is no more sickness inside you. The sickness is gone, yet the devil is still trying to make you feel the symptoms of your sickness. Most of the time he will do this by playing mind games with you, making what is not even real appear to be real. He's a skilled illusionist.

Don't worry about anything.

Many doctors have agreed that more than 65 percent of their patients' sicknesses are a direct result of mental reactions and instability within their nervous systems. Since the devil knows this, he'll try every method he can think of to make you believe that you are still sick when God has made you well.

I clearly remember when God healed me of tropical malaria. The enemy came to me on the very next day at 4 o'clock. He said, "I can tell that you are getting those headaches all over again, aren't you? Your back is beginning to hurt you badly. I think you had better get back in your bed. Any minute now you are going to have one of those major chills." I remember saying, "You're absolutely right—I am feeling some pain in my back." I took off my clothes, climbed into my bed, and patiently awaited my chills. I remember God asking me, "Why are you in bed?" I said, "Lord, I'm waiting for my chill to arrive."

He said, "Have you already forgotten that I healed you at two o'clock this morning?" "That's right, Lord; the

15

devil has me here waiting. He's using his wicked schemes and devices to put symptoms on me and discourage me. What do You want me to do, Lord?" God said, "Get up out of that bed, go down to the street corner, and preach." I obeyed God. I got up out of the bed, put my clothes on, went down to the street corner, and preached His Word.

Three people gave their lives to the Lord that day— and I was no longer bothered by the devil. All the symptoms left me. You see, I resisted the devil, and he had to flee out of my presence. Be careful for nothing. In other words, don't worry about anything. Just don't sweat it. Biblical faith is an action word that takes place in your spirit, not your emotions. It is with faith that man believes in God and is made righteous.

In the same way a person believes God for his or her healing, and healing comes. Since faith for healing is in your heart, do not allow the enemy to make you worry about whether or not you have actually received. When you worry over whether God's done it or not, you may lose your healing through doubt and unbelief, both of which are sins. Be careful for nothing. Continue to stand on what God's Word says. And, refuse to allow the enemy to change your mind concerning God's healing promise to you.

But what saith it? The word is nigh thee, even in thy mouth, and in thy heart: that is, the word of faith, which we preach; that if thou shalt confess with thy mouth the Lord Jesus, and shalt believe in thine heart that God hath raised him from the dead, thou shalt be saved. For with the heart man believeth unto righteousness; and with the mouth confession is made unto salvation (Romans 10:8-10).

Step #4: Forgive Those Who Have Wronged You

For if ye forgive men their trespasses, your heavenly Father will also forgive you: but if ye forgive not men their trespasses, neither will your Father forgive your trespasses (Matthew 6:14-15).

And when ye stand praying, forgive, if ye have ought against any: that your Father also which is in heaven may forgive you your trespasses. But if ye do not forgive, neither will your Father which is in heaven forgive your trespasses (Mark 11:25-26).

Under no circumstances will God give you the allowance not to forgive anyone. One of the chief reasons people do not receive their healing is because they continue to hold grudges in their hearts, unmercifully condemning their brothers or sisters to the point that God cannot extend His mercy on them. It does not take much to stop up the flow of God's healing virtue. Just one little grudge in your heart can separate you from God's healing touch.

Sad to say, I have heard Christians actually say, "I'll never forgive that person. I have a memory like an elephant. What they did to me is more than I'll ever be willing to forgive them for." Beware of making statements like these. Whoever makes statements like these is also making another statement—that person is saying that he or she is just the opposite of Jesus. The Scriptures tell us that all have sinned and fallen short of God's glory. However, God says of our sins, *"As far as the east is from the west, so far hath he removed our transgressions from us"* (Psalm 103:12).

Just one little grudge in your heart can separate you from God's healing touch.

If Jesus, who had no sin, can forget sins that we actually committed against Him, why is it so difficult for you to forgive your brother or sister who sinned against you? Every now and then the devil may come to you and say, "You don't have any right to God's blessings. Don't you remember what you did two days ago? Don't you remember how you allowed jealousy to enter into your heart about two months ago?" When this happens I tell folks to tell the devil, "I don't remember."

You may say, "Brother Coe, well, that's lying." No, my friend, I am not lying. If Jesus forgave my sins and refuses to remember them, then why should I? Why do I need to bring up old trash? It was done, it was wrong, but now it's over! The blood of Jesus has covered my sin. Every time God looks at me, He can't see any sin; all He sees is the blood of Jesus. So as far as God is concerned, I have every right to everything that any other believer has. It's not because of my good works but because of Jesus' blood sacrifice.

18

Some people feel as if they should put a number limit on forgiveness. They say, "I've forgiven a particular brother or sister more than ten times, and he or she just keeps on doing the same ol' thing. I am just sick and tired of that irresponsible behavior." Just suppose God acted the same way toward you. Suppose God said, "Jesus, I am ordering You not to forgive them seventy times seven times today, just twice. They acted like a bunch of idiots and they need to get their acts straight or else."

God's not like that. He is merciful toward us. We need to follow God's example more closely. The truth of the matter is that if you will not forgive your brother or your sister when he or she asks you, there will be a block, an obstacle, between you and the Lord. He cannot forgive your transgression and heal you until you first forgive others. He will not heal you as long as you are refusing to love others. You must make it a priority to love people above their faults and failures and forgive them quickly!

Step #5: Seek Christ and His Kingdom First, Not Healing

> *But seek ye first the kingdom of God, and his righteousness; and all these things shall be added unto you* (Matthew 6:33).

If you are seeking healing, I command you to stop now. Stop seeking your healing and instead seek the Christ who heals. In all things Christ is first. First is always His rightful place regardless of where we choose to put Him. Think of it like this. If there were a long line of people waiting to touch you, where would you want Jesus to be in that line? I would hope that Jesus would be in the front of the line, not second, third, or last. The closer that He is to you, the easier His loving hand can reach out to touch you. So you would naturally and intentionally place Jesus as close to you as possible.

Large numbers of people come out to my healing campaigns seeking their healing. That is really the only reason that some of them come. They don't come to worship and glorify God. Many of them are not really interested in basking in the presence of the Lord. They don't come to participate in giving. The only reason they come is to get healed. Many of them have already made up in their minds that, when they receive their healing, they are never going to come back to church ever again. If they got healed they would immediately return to the pleasures of this world, completely forgetting what God had done for them.

This type of behavior really grieves the Holy Spirit. It is indicative of an attitude of selfishness. You want God to give to you, but you can't give Him anything—not even a thank you. What you should do is seek the very source of healing, which is Jesus Christ. Healings come and healings go. However, Jesus Christ will always remain and will always be the same. He is the only one who is truly consistent in every era. Hebrews 13:8 declares, *"Jesus Christ the same yesterday, and to day, and for ever."*

Seek Christ who heals, not the healing.

Stop seeking the results and seek God. Your real goal should be to reach the place where you can honestly confess that you would rather have Jesus than silver or gold. You should be able to say that you would rather have Jesus than health or pleasure. If you present your body as a living sacrifice and allow Him to use you in any way that He sees fit for His kingdom, then and only then will you be in the rightful position to receive healing.

> *I beseech you therefore, brethren, by the mercies of God, that ye present your bodies a living sacrifice, holy, acceptable unto God, which is your reasonable service. And be not conformed to this world: but be ye transformed by the renewing of your mind, that ye may prove what is that good, and acceptable, and perfect, will of God* (Romans 12:1-2).

In seeking Christ you need to seek His Spirit. You need to ask Him to fill you up with His Holy Spirit so that your thoughts will be turned toward Jesus. (See Acts 1:8.) If you need healing in your body, you should seek Jesus. When you need financial help, does it make sense to pray for finances? No! You seek Jesus and ask Him to supply your needs. You must understand that Christ has everything that any one of us can need. It's on the inside of Him. In addition to that, He already knows what we need and has made provision for us.

> *And seek not ye what ye shall eat, or what ye shall drink, neither be ye of doubtful mind. For all these things do the nations of the world seek after: and your Father knoweth that ye have need of these things* (Luke 12:29-30).

When we seek Him, we in turn receive *all* that He has. The Bible says, *"**All** these things shall be added unto you"* (Matthew 6:33). *All* means that your cancers will be healed. It means that your blinded eyes will be made to see. *All* means that your finances will be increased. Your difficulties will be taken care of. Simply put, God is saying that if you seek Him first, He'll take care of everything else for you. You have nothing to worry about.

All of us desperately need to prioritize and reorder our lives. We must put our lives back in proper perspective. So many of us have our lives in wrong chronological order. That is the main reason things are not working the way we expected them to.

I've noticed that when people move to a new town or city they are first inclined to seek a job so they might secure a stable source of income. The next thing they do is seek out a house or apartment to live in. After that they seek out a good school system in the area to educate their children. When all those things are in place, then they start looking for a church home. Far too often I've seen people who follow this pattern, working so hard to pay the bills in their new house or apartment that they eventually backslide and never come to church anymore.

Had they put God first, *all these things would have been added to them.* This is God's promise to you. All of these things (the house, the car, the solid school system, the children's college education, the dream home) would have been added if they sought God first. They would have had not only the things, but also peace of mind with the hope of eternal life in the hereafter.

If you desire healing in your body, start seeking God. Tomorrow morning when you arise to pray, instead of praying, "Lord, heal my body," seek God. Tell God that you desire to have an intimate relationship and a closer walk with Him. Start your day with the expectation that you are going to be a lifestyle soul-winner. Remind God that you intend to live for Him with all your heart, mind, soul, and strength. I promise you that if you do those things and sincerely mean them from your heart, you will not want for any good thing. Jesus will meet all your needs.

Labour not for the meat which perisheth, but for that meat which endureth unto everlasting life, which the Son of man shall give unto you: for him hath God the Father sealed (John 6:27).

Chapter Two

Know That Healing Belongs to You

But unto you that fear my name shall the Sun of righteousness arise with healing in his wings; and ye shall go forth, and grow up as calves of the stall (Malachi 4:2).

But he was wounded for our transgressions, he was bruised for our iniquities: the chastisement of our peace was upon him; and with his stripes we are healed (Isaiah 53:5).

In order to receive your healing, you will have to get rid of some erroneous theology that you may have been taught. This wrong teaching espouses a doctrine that makes you accommodate sickness in your body. It makes you feel comfortable with being sick. If you are

25

comfortable with being sick, you will never be healed. You have to become totally adverse toward sickness. You've heard this teaching before. It says that everybody has to get sick; sometimes it's only natural. Nothing could be further from the truth. Although this concept may be the conventional thinking about healing, it totally opposes what God's Word has to say on the matter.

According to God's Word, healing belongs to the children of God. It's our rightful portion. You've got to believe this. Now, you may tell me that everybody has to die some time or another. Personally, I believe that we may very well be the generation that will be alive when Jesus returns for His bride. Even if you did happen to die, you don't necessarily have to get sick and then die. The Lord Jesus can simply say, "It's time to go now. Come on up a littler higher." When you close your eyes shut and open them again, suddenly you will discover that you are in the presence of your Savior.

Realize that Jesus came to rid the world of pain, sorrow, and sickness—all of which are by-products of sin. Just look around and it will become more and more obvious to you that the human race is heavily afflicted by all of these. So in order to be healed, you have to see yourself as being freed from sickness and diseases. Those things belong to the devil, and he is the one who should have them.

Cataracts, cancers and other encumbering diseases are all going to be miraculously healed by Jesus long before He comes back for His church. In the same way that God sovereignly used Moses to deliver the children of Israel out of Egyptian bondage and slavery, He is using people with a message of healing to free us from the thought patterns of this world that keep us under the bondage of sickness and disease.

> *And thou shalt say unto him, The LORD God of the Hebrews hath sent me unto thee, saying, Let my people go, that they may serve me in the wilderness: and, behold, hitherto thou wouldest not hear* (Exodus 7:16).

By the authority of Jesus Christ, I command the enemy to let you go. "Satan, let God's people go! Loose them from the false teaching about healing that has kept them bound and sick. Loose them from the wrong belief that God does not care whether or not they are healed. Loose them from the mentality that believes healing is for every-one else, yet not for them. Satan, let God's people go who wrongly believe that He wants them to be sick so He can get glory from their sickness. Let God's people go who believe that sickness should be an accepted way of living. In the name of Jesus, LET HIS PEOPLE GO!"

You've got kingdom business to tend to. God has pre-pared a sumptuous feast in the wilderness and invited you as His special guest. The problem is that you cannot come to the table until you get freed from Satan's decep-tive clutch. Knowledge of Christ's Word is the key that will progressively free you.

As we come into the knowledge of God's true will for our lives, we recognize that it is God's desire for us to embrace the healing message. Once we do, there won't be any blinded eyes or crippled limbs, and cancer will become a historical word. You may be thinking that I'm describing life after Jesus has raptured us. That's not when I am talking about.

Long before Jesus returns we will experience—as one unified body—complete wholeness. The Bible lets us know that Jesus Christ is coming back for a *glorious* church, not a sick and diseased, tattered and torn church. Once you believe that healing is for you right now, you will begin to walk in the ways that God Himself has prepared for you—the good life.

That he might present it to himself a glorious church, not having spot, or wrinkle, or any such thing; but that it should be holy and without blemish (Ephesians 5:27).

Understanding the Three Kinds of Healing

It is important to know that God has different methods He uses to heal His people. He will not always use the same method that He used in prior times to show forth His power today. One reason He won't do things the same way all the time is so man cannot force God into a box. He refuses to dance to our tune. The reason for this is very elementary: He is God and He can choose to heal however He would like to.

So in order to understand healing we first have to understand the three different ways that it may come. One way healing can come is gradually, or in time.

Another way of looking at gradual healing is by understanding that healing has a progressive dimension to it, meaning that it can happen in stages much like a building is built. A tall building is never built in an instant; it is built in many stages. The foundation alone takes time in order to settle properly. To rush the process may cause the foundation or other parts of the building to be improperly installed.

Other times healing will happen in an instant. Then there are times when your faith will activate your healing.

Although God is not limited to these three forms of healing, these are the three ways that He has chosen to use. I realize that God in His matchless wisdom and might can employ another method without any given notice. The bottom line is, whichever of these methods He chooses to use, you will still receive your healing.

Gradual Healing

And as he entered into a certain village, there met him ten men that were lepers, which stood afar off: and they lifted up their voices, and said, Jesus, Master, have mercy on us. And when he saw them, he said unto them, Go show yourselves unto the priests. And it came to pass, that, as they went, they were cleansed (Luke 17:12-14).

Some people quickly become discouraged when they don't receive their healing immediately. I have heard people who came to my healing campaigns complain because they did not receive their healing immediately after they had been prayed for. Some became bitter and disgruntled. The worse thing, though, is that they began to speak negative words about healing. They'd say, "I'm never going to be healed. Surely, I'll die now. I knew that I should have never gone to the service in the first place."

Words like these only worsen your situation. What these people did not realize is just because they did not receive the physical manifestation of healing in their body did not mean that they were not healed. They were looking at the symptoms, as I discussed earlier. They also were looking for a sign and not looking to the Word of God that has already declared they are free in Jesus' name. Since they did not receive the physical proof of their healing, they ignorantly thought that they were not healed.

Their negative attitude combined with their negative words caused them to abort their healing altogether. How unfortunate! If only they had realized that not all healings come in an instant, then they would not have been discouraged by the progressing results. The Bible records the story of the ten lepers. The Scripture declare that Jesus healed all ten. However, the Scriptures also let us know that they were healed "as they went," not immediately. That phrase, "as they went," suggests that their cleansing came in stages, but progress was continual and steady.

Think about it this way. You can travel from Dallas, Texas, to Philadelphia, Pennsylvania, several different ways. One way is to travel by a jet plane. This means of travel will get you to your destination the quickest way.

However, some people who like to view the scenery of the country will travel by an automobile. Both methods will get you to your destination. They both accomplish the same goal. One method is just not as quick as the other.

A plane is no better than a car. Although planes cost far more than your average car, a car has far more usefulness and greater applications than an airplane does. An airplane is just different. So realize first that God may not always heal in an instant, but He may heal you gradually. And if that is how God chooses to operate, accept it and be thankful.

If God heals you gradually, be thankful!

That brings me to another point. These ten lepers were miraculously, yet progressively, healed by the power of Jesus. Out of ten lepers you would think that common courtesy would cause all of them to show gratitude. For the sake of averages, even if half of the lepers came back to offer thanks it would have been a good start.

The Scriptures tell us that only one leper had the heart to come back and tell Jesus thank you. This lack of gratitude is yet another reason so many people are disqualified from receiving an instant miracle. Their selfish actions and attitude of ungratefulness are clear indications of how much worse their behavior would have been had they received their total healing in an instant.

By an Act of Faith

The second way God heals is through the act of faith. The Bible says in Hebrews 11:6, *"But without faith it is impossible to please him: for he that cometh to God must believe that he is, and that he is a rewarder of them that diligently seek him."* Faith is something that God always has and always will respond to. The Bible says that we cannot even accomplish the simple goal of pleasing God unless we respond in faith and live by faith.

No matter what God is doing, He will always respond to our situation if we are acting in faith. The problem is that many people don't really understand what biblical faith is. Biblical faith is believing so strongly in what God's Word says that you take action to prove that you believe it. If you don't take action, then you probably don't have real faith. I know that may sound hard, but it's true nonetheless. A classic example of this can be seen in the story of the woman who had an issue of blood.

God will always respond to faith.

According to the Bible, this woman suffered with a continuous hemorrhaging for 12 years. Twelve days would be too long for any person to suffer with a bleeding problem, wouldn't you agree? This woman suffered for far longer than that. She had spent money with the best physicians in her region trying to discover a cure to her problem. She had spent all that she had, but her problem only worsened. The doctors did not have any answers for her or a favorable outlook.

At this point this woman felt as if her only option was to believe God. Undoubtedly, her fellow community members had already ostracized her. Her family and friends could not have any real physical contact with her since she was ceremonially unclean. If she had children, they would not have been allowed to see their mother. So in many ways this woman may have felt as if she was already dead and gone.

This situation only put this woman in a position to desperately seek God. Often when you seem as if you don't have any more options, God becomes your only recourse. It's either God or death. That has to be your mind-set if you choose to operate in faith. When this woman heard that Jesus was in the crowd, she took her chances to act in faith by touching the hem of His garment.

For she said within herself, If I may but touch his garment, I shall be whole. But Jesus turned him about, and when he saw her, he said, Daughter, be of good comfort; thy faith hath made thee whole. And the woman was made whole from that hour (Matthew 9:21-22).

This woman needed no further convincing. She had already concluded within herself that if she could touch the garment of Jesus, she would receive a total and complete healing. She needed neither a private audience nor a counseling session with Jesus. She did not have to physically touch His flesh. Whether Jesus laid His hands on her head or her uterus area did not matter. She knew that if she could just touch the hem of Jesus' garment, she would be whole.

Although she could have been literally killed in the process, this woman successfully touched the hem of

Jesus' garment. Jesus told her that her act of faith made her well. Interestingly, in this situation the Bible does not say that it was Christ' anointing that healed this woman, but rather her own faith. God is always waiting for you to do something out of the ordinary. He is just waiting for you to respond in faith to your deepest heart's conviction. If you really believe, then prove that you believe. Do something and watch God do the rest!

Instantaneous Healing

The final way that God heals is in an instant. Although He does not heal instantly every single time, He does use this method on a very consistent basis. During my healing campaigns I have seen God heal all three ways. However, I have seen perhaps more instantaneous healings than any other kind. The reason I believe God uses this method so often is because it really does not involve human action but relies totally on God's judgment and mercy combined.

A classic example of this is recorded in the gospel of Mark, the second chapter. Jesus was returning again into Capernaum. Every person got the news that Jesus was coming to town. The word spread so fast that people who wanted to see Jesus literally packed out the house where He was lodging. There wasn't even standing room inside the house. Jesus began to preach to them. While Jesus was in the middle of His message, five latecomers showed up for the service.

These latecomers consisted of one crippled and paralyzed man and his four friends who brought him to be healed. (This story also has a strong and clear definition on what a true friend is from what a friend is not. True friends will always look out for your best interest, not theirs.) Since they arrived so late and the service was so packed, they could not get into the house. This crippled man's friends were so determined to get inside where Jesus was that they literally dug through the clay roof and made an opening large enough to lower their friend through it.

Instantaneous healings do not involve human action but rely totally on God.

Obviously this obnoxious act of faith interrupted the entire meeting. However, Jesus was so impressed with their act of faith that He told the sick man that his sins were forgiven. The religious folks who heard Jesus say this got so upset that they began to accuse Him of blaspheming against God. They felt as if He had no right or authority to forgive anyone's sin; only God could do that. Jesus proceeded to inform them that He was the Messiah and because of that He could forgive sin on earth. He had that right.

Since Jesus knew that they probably did not believe what He was claiming, He decided to perform a miracle to prove to the religious leaders that He was who He claimed to be. I believe that in many cases God will use us to perform His miracles so that unbelievers and doubters will believe as a result because of the unarguable proof.

35

I say unto thee, Arise, and take up thy bed, and go thy way into thine house. And immediately he arose, took up the bed, and went forth before them all; insomuch that they were all amazed, and glorified God, saying, We never saw it on this fashion (Mark 2:11-12).

The Bible says that this man *immediately* rose up, took up his bed, and starting walking. He received an instantaneous healing. There is nowhere in this scripture passage that lets us know whether or not this man exercised his own faith. We do know that this healing was not a gradual one because the Bible says he immediately rose up. It is very interesting that his friends were the ones who had faith, and yet he got healed. God is always looking for opportunities to heal instantaneously to prove the He is exactly who He says He is—Jehovah Raffa, God Our Healer. I suggest that you remain in God's clear-eye view because it is very possible that you might be next in line for an instantaneous healing.

Why Are Not All Healings Instantaneous?

So Naaman came with his horses and with his chariot, and stood at the door of the house of Elisha. And Elisha sent a messenger unto him, saying, Go and wash in Jordan seven times, and thy flesh shall come again to thee, and thou shalt be clean. But Naaman was wroth, and went away, and said, Behold, I thought, He will surely come out to me, and stand, and call on the name of the LORD his God, and strike his hand over the place, and recover the leper (2 Kings 5:9-11).

Not all healings are instantaneous because there are lessons that may never be learned if your healing came too quickly. This does not necessarily apply to everyone. However, there are some people who would not properly benefit from having an immediate healing and, in fact, their healing could become a curse instead of a blessing to them.

The Bible says that Naaman was the captain of the Syrian army. He had great favor in the eyes of the Syrian king. And since he was such a great leader and warrior, the people of Syria celebrated him. Added to the great list of Naaman's accolades was the fact that he was a leper. Leprosy was a progressive, infectious disease that caused the flesh to form white, scaly, puss-like scabs. In one sense it was a type of flesh-eating disease. For the most part this disease was associated with the lower class and poor people during that time. It was a disease that would cause other people to look down on you if you contracted it.

Since Naaman was so popular with the people and the king, he began to believe that the God of Israel should grant him a private audience and heal him. At the very least he thought that God should have dispatched one of His most skilled healers to wave his hand over him and he's instantly be healed. Because of his status, he sincerely believed that he was entitled to special privileges. God intentionally did not choose any of those methods. Rather, God chose to use the least likely person to communicate a message to Naaman, a message

37

that would cause Naaman to begin embracing the spirit of humility; hence his lesson was begun.

The story all started with a Hebrew maidservant of Naaman's wife. This girl was a servant class citizen, which was just above being a slave. For the most part masters totally ignored whatever suggestions their servants would make. In many cases the servants were there only to serve and do what they were told to do. They usually were not allowed to even offer suggestions, as that may have jeopardized their job. This Israeli maidservant, however, told Naaman's wife that she knew a prophet in Israel who could perform miracles, and if her master could get an audience with him, she knew that the prophet would be able to heal Naaman.

Naaman wanted to get rid of this leprous stigma so badly that he consulted with the king of Syria and shared the information that this girl told him. The Syrian king gave Naaman a letter to bring to the king of Israel as an introduction. When the king of Israel read the letter, he thought it was just another ruse for the Syrian army to invade Israel again. But Elisha the prophet learned of the situation and asked the king to send Naaman to him. He realized that Naaman's situation did not warrant a king but rather a prophet of the Lord.

As was customary, Naaman brought nearly $100,000 as an offering to give to the king. It is always in order to bring a gift when you are going to make an inquiry. However, in this case no gift would be acceptable in exchange for Naaman's healing. Naaman had to go through a deduction process in order to see how big and powerful God really is. His stature, status, fame, and accomplishments could not do anything to heal him. Those things helped him to advance in other areas, but not in God's kingdom. His obedience and humility to follow the orders of the prophet would eventually heal him, but it would take time.

The Bible says that Elisha asked Naaman to dip in the nastiest, filthiest river in that region, the Jordan River. Immediately Naaman's pride made him feel as if he was too good to dip seven times in the river. After all, he was the Syrian king's right-hand man. Eventually he conceded to dip in this dirty river. After the seventh time, Naaman's skin was completely cleansed from leprosy. Had he only dipped six times and not seven, he would have never received his healing.

I believe that if God had healed Naaman immediately, he would have been caught up in pride and arrogance, believing that it was position that caused God healed him. Some people who are against offerings use this verse to justify their cheap and stingy ways. They say, "Elisha did not receive an offering from Naaman, so why should you, Brother Coe?" You have got to see that this situation was expressly different.

God forbade Elisha to receive from Naaman because Naaman would have become confused and thought that his money bought him a miracle. To end that potential confusion of thought, it was easier for Elisha not to accept that offering *from him*. However, Elisha knew that God was his source and that whatever he was willing to walk away from would inevitably determine what God would bring into his life.

So for Naaman and anyone like him, God may not heal as quickly as you believe He should. Often in life there are valuable lessons we must accept in order to grow to the next level of spiritual maturity. If we do not, we will inevitably repeat the same cycles over and over again. Learn your lesson.

Jesus Is Still Healing the Same Three Ways Today

Years ago, I was riding in a car with my former campaign manager and we were talking about things that had happened in the past. I remember him asking me, "Do you remember the time in Beaumont, Texas, when you prayed for an old man who was about seventy years old at the time? Do you remember how he was healed instantly and began walking all around the tent?" I began to remember exactly the man he was referring to. This same man, after he was healed, started walking between three to four miles every day—something that he would have only dreamed of doing while in his crippled state.

On the edge of the platform at the church that I pastor, Dallas Revival Center, is a scar in the plaster. That scar is from the crutches that were put there by a young crippled man who faithfully attended my Bible classes Sunday after Sunday. Every Sunday I had to look at him in his crippled condition while I preached the message of deliverance with great conviction. While preaching one day, my mind reverted back to this old man who was healed in the Beaumont, Texas, healing campaign.

I began to think about the fact that this man in my church was a young man with great possibilities and the potential for a great future ahead of him. I thought about the fact that this old man was instantly healed and that he (the old man) had not even heard but one Gospel message on healing. The younger man had heard several messages on healing and deliverance, yet had never released his faith to receive. I felt that if God could heal the old man, He could also heal the younger man.

I started to get mad. While I was preaching, I looked directly at the young man and said, "You are a disgrace to my church!" I told him, "I've been preaching healing and deliverance and there you sit week after week with those crutches. I want you to get up right now and let me pray for you." When he was almost to the front, I prayed for him. I took the man's crutches and broke them in two pieces. Without more ado, he began to shout, run, and jump hysterically up and down the aisles. God had healed him immediately, in an instant.

It's unfortunate but it's true that God cannot heal everybody instantly. Some folks would backslide and never do anything for God if they were healed instantly. Others would go back into the same restrictive sins that once enslaved them. So for some people their afflictions are the only places where they will seek God. And seeking God is a good thing. David said in Psalm 119:71, *"It is good for me that I have been afflicted; that I might learn thy statutes."*

41

Some people just won't seek God until they are on the bed of affliction.

Some people work so hard just to make ends meet that they are carried away by the cares of this life and don't have time to pray, read the Bible, and wait on the Lord. One night a woman came running up to me in a tent crusade and cried out, "We've driven all the way from Oklahoma to be healed. We want you to heal every one of us. We have to get back tonight." I looked at this sister and asked, "Well, sister, can't you stay any longer? I believe that if you stay around this anointed atmosphere just a little while longer that you will receive your healing."

God cannot heal everyone instantly because it might be detrimental for them.

I told her, "If you went to the hospital and needed to be thoroughly examined by the doctor, you wouldn't just run out until you've had a thorough examination." She told me, "Brother Coe, you just don't understand. I don't have time to stay any longer. I'm a real busy lady and I have a whole lot of things to do. I'm sort of in a hurry."

Although this lady's story may sound unique, really it is not. The entire world is in such a rush and a hurry that everyone seems to be a bit confused. When we become so busy that we don't have time for God, we suddenly realize that His shadow is far removed from us. When that happens, the devil has free range to do whatever he desires to do to us. That's how cancer, heart disease, and kidney failures often occur. When people choose every-thing else over spending quality time with God, healing doesn't happen easily.

God at times will use gradual healing to cause us to realize that we must continually walk with Him. He desires us to draw closer to Him and fellowship with Him. Jackie Rhodes, who we will talk about later, was healed from a disease called scleroderma. However, she was not healed instantly. Scleroderma is a disease of unknown causes that makes the skin get hard and thick due to abnormalities in the fibrous tissues. After she was prayed for and received her healing, little by little the old black, dead skin on her body began to disappear. She began to use her stiffened limbs once more. Did it hap-pen overnight? No. But what she learned throughout her healing process was of more value than the healing itself.

I was holding a revival in Pampa, Texas. A man came in the service and asked whose car was blocking the door. I told him it was my car. He asked me if I could move the car so that he could wheel his wife on her med-ical bed into the church. He thought it would make it a whole lot easier after the service was over if I just moved my car before the service got too involved. His wife had been paralyzed for 12 years. I didn't really mind moving my car, but I asked him, "Why don't you just believe that God will heal your wife and then she could walk out of the service on her own without you having to carry her?"

He told me, "Please just move your car, sir. I've taken my wife to every healing evangelist in the country and every medical specialist that deals with her illness. She hasn't gotten a bit better. Please just move your car and you can park in my space." I went out and moved my car as the gentlemen asked. I really didn't know why he came to the service in the first place if he wasn't going to believe God for his wife to be healed. Frankly, I thought that he was wasting his and his wife's time.

He wheeled his wife in and propped her up on the bed. Several of the sisters in the church went over to the lady, who was very obviously maimed, and began to pray for her intensely. Honestly, I did not think that she was going to be healed. I didn't think that the atmosphere was right, and I definitely knew that her husband's attitude was all wrong.

But there was this old lady who began to pray for this woman. She said these words: "Lord, I am old now and I don't have much time to live anyway, so for the sake of your Son Jesus please heal this young woman." She wanted God to give this woman the opportunity to live out her life with meaning. God miraculously healed this woman because of this unknown older lady's sincere prayer.

There are a lot of people who look at Brother Freeman, Brother Roberts, and myself and think that people are always healed because of our faith. That's not always so. You would be totally amazed how often someone who looks totally unassuming in the congregation has released his or her faith for another person's healing and God honors it. God uses many ways to heal, but in the final analysis He gets all the glory!

Chapter Three

Faith With Works, Works!

Yea, a man may say, Thou hast faith, and I have works: show me thy faith without thy works, and I will show thee my faith by my works. Thou believest that there is one God; thou doest well: the devils also believe, and tremble. But wilt thou know, O vain man, that faith without works is dead? (James 2:18-20).

I want to deal with an area of great controversy concerning faith and the working of miracles. There have been some ministers who unfortunately do not live very moral lifestyles yet, when they get in the pulpit, preach God's Word, and pray for the sick, miracles happen. The power of God miraculously heals people. They literally live like the devil all week long, then when the time for ministering comes, God seems to honor them. Now I am not in any way, shape, or form condoning immoral behavior—especially among preachers.

If anyone should live a lifestyle exemplary of Jesus Christ, it is preachers. The point I am making, however, is that miracles do not occur because of the man who is preaching faith. Obviously the miracle cannot be credited to his bawdy lifestyle. So if it's not the man's faith that is working on behalf of the sick person, then whose faith is it? I believe that those miracles take place because God is working on the behalf of the faith of the people in the congregation and the faith of the people who brought the sick to the service.

Their act of faith in bringing their sick friend or loved one to the place where God's Word is proclaimed is the action necessary to produce healing results in the life of the sick or diseased person. Why does it work this way? First, God always honors people who act in faith and validate their faith with corresponding actions. Secondly, God has some rules that He set up for Himself that are literally impossible to break. He cannot go against His Word. It's absolutely impossible!

The Bible tells us that heaven and earth will be ended—or demolished, for that matter—before God does not honor His Word. God and His Word are divinely one. Matthew 5:18 says, *"For verily I say unto you, Till heaven and earth pass, one jot or one tittle shall in no wise pass from the law, till all be fulfilled."* God and His Word are inseparable. And that cannot change.

Since His Word cannot change, then we've got to accept what His Word says about why signs and wonders happen. The Bible says, *"And they went forth, and preached every where, the Lord working with them, and confirming the word with signs following. Amen"* (Mark 16:20). This scripture is living proof that God confirms His Word with signs and wonders. It doesn't matter who preaches the Word. It only matters that the Word is being preached. Although it may sound a little absurd, even if the devil preached God's Word in hell, signs and wonders would follow. It's God's Word.

You may ask, "Brother Coe, why is it that every church in America and all over the world is not experiencing the manifestation of the healing power of God? When I travel around the United States, I see sick people in most churches that I go to. I'm sure that they are preaching the Word, so why aren't the people in those churches getting healed and set free by the power of God?" I am so glad you asked that question.

Just because you have a church and a congregation with a pastor over it does not mean that the pastor is preaching and teaching the Word of God. There are thousands of pastors who don't even believe in healing. I covered that earlier. Thousands more totally reject the belief in a God who works miracles. Do you think that someone who doesn't believe in healing will actually preach on healing? Absolutely not! You can only preach on what you are convicted of. And if you don't hold a personal conviction about something, you can't preach about it.

47

That's why so many churchgoers will go to heaven when they die, yet live this life in an earthly hell. Their bodies are so racked with sickness and pain that they can barely stand up. They can hardly function from day to day. Yet they continue to faithfully attend the dead church where there are more deaths and funerals than there are people getting saved.

If some preachers aren't preaching the Word of God that produces signs and wonders, then what are they preaching? Some are preaching their opinions. Others are preaching man's philosophy. Many denominations teach their young preachers to preach their rules and regulations. Some people preach their wrong interpretations of the Scriptures. There are a whole bunch of other things that people preach. I do not have time to list them all.

However, if you preach the Word, you will always get results—no matter who you are. Now for all you know-it-alls, "think you are so smart" theologians who are saying that's not biblical, you must understand that God never says in His Word that if you preach His Word He will confirm you. He doesn't confirm the person. If He confirms the individual, He would almost be justifying whatever wrongs they committed.

He doesn't confirm the person; He confirms His Word. And the very act of preaching God's Word is an action of faith. Believe me when I tell you that it takes action to preach the uncompromising, unadulterated Word of the living God. When the Word of God is preached, the captives are set free. They are overjoyed. On the other side, the devil and all his groupies are totally outraged. So the devil will do everything in his power to stop you from taking action. He knows that actions of faith work, especially the preaching and teaching of God's Word.

Working Faith

You've got to put your faith to work. The Bible says, *"Even so faith, if it hath not works, is dead, being alone"* (James 2:17). There is no such thing as real faith unless it is attached to an action. If you really have biblical faith, you'll always be inclined to do something to demonstrate your faith. The problem is that most people—ministers included—are scared stiff to do things that the majority of people might think is a bit unethical by their standards (not God's).

Most people try to shy away from the image that people will have of them if they do what God says to do. I'm sorry to tell you that you will never do anything worthwhile for God if you have that poor and wimpy attitude. When God infuses your soul with faith and His power to do the miraculous, you are going to be a very visible target for the enemy—all the time. God will ask you to do things that are controversial. He will put you right out there to be criticized.

God does this for two reasons. The first is that God can't do anything great unless you take the action to do something strange. Second, God wants to establish between you and Him that the opinions of no one else in the world matter to you more than God's. What God says means more than anything to you, and that settles it. That's the kind of bold and committed attitude that God is looking for you to have.

That brings to my mind a meeting a few years ago that I was in with Brother Oral Roberts in Miami, Florida. I was sitting on the platform with local ministers and a few other guest clergymen. There were long lines of people patiently waiting for Brother Roberts to pray for them. A man who was a deaf mute was next up to be prayed for. Although I was sitting close enough to where Brother Roberts was praying and could clearly see what he was doing, I almost had to look twice after I realized what he was doing.

Real faith is attached to an action.

Brother Roberts was actually spitting in his hands. He was filling the palms of his hands with his spit. At first I did not know what in the world he was doing. But then it hit me: God is going to use something real strange, an act of faith, to get this man healed. When the man came up to him, Brother Roberts said to the man, "Please, sir, stick out your tongue." The man looked a bit empty and puzzled. Yet he conceded.

When the man stuck out his tongue, Oral took hold of it and smeared the spit in his hands on it. There were two aristocratic older ladies who were sitting close to where I was seated. I heard them saying to one another, "Isn't that a GERMY thing to do?" The man who was a deaf mute amazingly began to speak and to hear. He had received his healing because Brother Roberts was not afraid to act in faith when other people thought that his actions were pretty nasty. That did not matter to him.

Brother Roberts' primary concern was to get this man healed. The way that it happened was not necessarily the most sanitary or even sensible way. However, God used this man's act of faith to bring about a miraculous healing in this deaf mute. What Oral did was an act of faith. There are many negative things that could have happened because of his actions. The whole audience could have thought that what he did was so inappropriate that they all got up and left. When you are acting in faith, you'll just take those kinds of chances, particularly when you know that it's God who is speaking to you.

During one of my healing campaigns in Binghamton, New York, a woman was standing in line with two people on either side of her, holding her feet securely in place. This woman had been diagnosed with a very terminal form of stomach cancer. Even while she was standing in the line I could tell that she was in excruciating pain in her abdomen area. As I was getting ready to lay my hands on her, I heard the Spirit of the Lord say, "Smite the cancer."

I thought, *Lord, do You really want me to punch this woman in the stomach in front of all of these witnesses?* I realized that God was trying to get me to take an action of ridiculous faith so that this woman could get her healing. With all my might I punched this small-framed lady in the stomach with my fist. The woman doubled over in pain. The devil said, "You've done it now. You've gone too far." I actually assaulted an innocent woman. Or did I?

God told me to pull the woman up and straighten her out. Then He told me to hit her again. Her stomach was obviously swollen and bloated—so much so that she had to wear a skirt that was at least six sizes larger than her normal frame just to fit around her cancer-filled stomach. When I hit her the second time, her stomach immediately became deflated. It almost looked like a flat tire. Her skirt fell down to her knees and she frantically started to pull her skirt back up. All the pain had completely gone away. She was miraculously healed by the power of God.

How did her healing happen? Was it an accident? Or was it a mere coincidence? It was none of those. This miracle happened because I stepped out in faith and obeyed what I knew God was telling me to do regardless of the apparent risks. When God tells you to do something, don't stand there arguing with God. Just do whatever He tells you to do. Just do it!

There have been many times when people who came to my crusades came with crutches and wheelchairs. The Lord told me to break the crutches or throw the wheelchair. The devil would always remind me that if these people did not get their healing, they wouldn't have any aids to help them walk and get around. That did not matter to me. I broke those crutches and then threw those wheelchairs. I can't remember one person who was not healed when God told me to do those things. Because I acted in faith, God showed Himself strong and mighty. He did it then and He'll do it again when you decide to get your faith to working.

Open Up Your Soul to God

In every generation you will always have skeptics and critics of faith and the power of God. Most of them are disguised as believers. But you and I both know that they really don't believe; they are simply religious. They'll say that in this dispensation miracles and healings do not happen as they did in Bible times anymore. They are absolutely wrong, my brother and sister. God's outpouring today will be even greater than it was in Bible days.

One day I asked God what the difference is between the last-day outpouring and the first as seen with Peter, James, and John. God asked me, "Jack, when you were a child, what was the first thing you looked for when you turned your eyes toward the stars?" I said, "Why, I always looked for the little dipper." Then God said, "What was the next thing you looked for?" I said, "The big dipper, Lord."

God said, "The first outpouring of My Spirit is like the emptying out of the little dipper. The last outpouring is like the emptying out of the big dipper. My Spirit will come down like rain." In this last move of God, I believe that people will get healed by our shadows in the same way that He used Peter's shadow to heal when he walked down the streets. I believe we can use Peter and John as our examples and follow the same authority they had when they spoke words of power and authority.

Now Peter and John went up together into the temple at the hour of prayer, being the ninth hour. And a certain man lame from his mother's womb

53

was carried, whom they laid daily at the gate of the temple which is called Beautiful, to ask alms of them that entered into the temple; who seeing Peter and John about to go into the temple asked an alms. And Peter, fastening his eyes upon him with John, said, Look on us. And he gave heed unto them, expecting to receive something of them. Then Peter said, Silver and gold have I none; but such as I have give I thee: In the name of Jesus Christ of Nazareth rise up and walk. And he took him by the right hand, and lifted him up: and immediately his feet and ankle bones received strength (Acts 3:1-7).

This story of Peter and John's Christ-like authority is a story that should not be unique to you. It should be your everyday reality. I believe with my whole heart that we the believers have this same authority and power today. If you have been baptized in the Holy Ghost, then you have access to the same power that I do. *"But ye shall receive **power**, after that the Holy Ghost is come upon you: and ye shall be witnesses unto me both in Jerusalem, and in all Judaea, and in Samaria, and unto the uttermost part of the earth"* (Acts 1:8). God is not a respecter of persons. However, He has and always will acknowledge people whose hearts are wide open to Him.

If you are hiding sin in your life, then your heart is not wide open to Him. If you have doubt and disbelief, then your heart is not wide open to Him. If you are timid about doing whatever He asks you to do, then your heart is not wide open to Him. God can use you to do great things for Him no matter what denomination or church group you belong to. All you have to do is open up your heart to Him and let Him fill it up with everything you will need in order to get His job accomplished.

You Must Have Clean Hands and a Clean Heart

He that hath clean hands, and a pure heart; who hath not lifted up his soul unto vanity, nor sworn deceitfully. He shall receive the blessing from the LORD, and righteousness from the God of his salvation (Psalm 24:4-5).

If you want your actions of faith to always work and be unhindered, you must receive your help from the Lord. You have got to pray through to God, asking Him to cleanse your heart from all unrighteousness. There is one prayer that I personally pray every single morning. It is, "God, forgive me, search me, and help me to have a pure heart."

The last time I said that publicly, someone came up to me afterwards and said, "Do you mean that Christians, filled with the Holy Ghost, can have impurities in their hearts?" I answered that person, "Yes. It can and does happen." The Bible says, *"If my people, which are called by my name, shall humble themselves, and pray, and seek my face, and turn from their wicked ways; then will I hear from heaven, and will forgive their sin, and will heal their land"* (2 Chronicles 7:14). Notice that this scripture does not say, "if my sinners" or "if my enemies," but rather "*if my people.*" *My people* refers to God's people who stand in need of repenting and searching.

If you are not a Christian, you are a child of the devil. However, there are times when a Christian can and does commit a sin. The Bible even bears this truth. First John 2:1-2 declares, *"My little children, these things write I unto you, that ye sin not. And if any man sin, we have an advocate with the Father, Jesus Christ the righteous: and he is the propitiation for our sins: and not for ours only, but also for the sins of the whole world."* I have heard people say, "I haven't sinned in thirty years." The person who says that is telling a blatant lie.

Even Christians sin and need forgiveness.

If we say that we have not sinned, we make him a liar, and his word is not in us (1 John 1:10).

If you really were to be truthful about it, you'd have to admit that the devil really hasn't left you alone since the day you got saved. Whether you want to believe it or not, he will continue to tempt you until you die. I'll be honest enough to admit that I'm constantly having trouble with Jack Coe. I am always saying things I shouldn't say and doing things I shouldn't do. What am I to do? Should I get discouraged and give up? Absolutely not! I'll never give the devil that pleasure.

I'm going to fall on my knees and say, "Lord, I've failed You. Please let Your blood cover my sins and failures. Let Your blood cover everything and make me clean again." When God looks at me from that point on, He doesn't see my sin or my stupid mistake. He only sees the blood of His Son Jesus. If you believe that you have sin in your life that is hindering you from acting on your faith, why don't you get down on your knees right now and ask God for His forgiveness?

After you have done that, get up and shout. Get up and begin to shout the victory and forget about it! If God has promised to forget your sins and remove them far from you, why do you worry about them anymore? Just let God put them all under the blood and move on. We've got too much work to do to allow an unclean heart and unclean hands to stop us. Get cleansed now by the blood of Jesus.

As far as the east is from the west, so far hath he removed our transgressions from us (Psalm 103:12).

Allowing Faith to Replace Your Fears

If you want to do great things for God or if you want God to do great things for you, you have to get rid of the spirit of fear. Fear will cause your faith not to work since it always impedes action and progress. Sad to say, many people in the body of Christ live in a constant state of fear. Some Christians don't live their life for Christ with great joy. They are scared because they believe they won't hold out until the end. They believe they will make some dumb mistake that will cause God to cast them away.

Fear makes people become paranoid. Some people believe that little sore on their face will become cancerous.

Others have a gas attack and believe they are dying with a heart attack. Little do they know that that kind of attack is caused from overeating, not a heart problem. But fear makes you always think the worst of everything. Once the devil convinces you of his lies concerning your health, you will live in a constant state of being tormented. That's exactly where he wants you—in a place where you take no action. You do absolutely nothing.

I know of people who, although they have been saved, believe that they are not right with God. The devil makes them think that they won't be caught up in the rapture when Jesus comes back again. Because you don't cast down such a wicked thought, like a seed that thought begins to grow. When it is grown starts to become your reality. Then you start saying, "I guess I am not saved. There's really no need to pray; God's not going to hear me anyway." Once you believe that, you're not going to be any good.

About six months after I got saved I did something wrong. I started going around with a long face. Being a baby Christian I did not realize that I was already forgiven just for the asking. Instead I would ask every preacher to lay his or her hands on me to get this spirit off of me. I wanted to *feel* forgiven. I should have simply stood on the Word of God, which declares my forgiven state. Each time I was prayed for, I would speak in tongues and shout the victory.

But when that joyous feeling was gone, the devil would return and put doubts in my mind all over again. He was trying to convince me that God no longer wanted to use me and that my mistake was so big (although it wasn't) that Jesus' blood was just not strong enough to cleanse me. Although the Bible totally opposes this attitude, I was outright scared. If only I had known these scriptures:

For God hath not given us the spirit of fear; but of power, and of love, and of a sound mind (2 Timothy 1:7).

For ye have not received the spirit of bondage again to fear; but ye have received the Spirit of adoption, whereby we cry, Abba, Father. The Spirit itself beareth witness with our spirit, that we are the children of God (Romans 8:15-16).

Then I discovered the truth of God. I began to realize that what God did for Job, He had done for me; He had built a hedge of protection around me. I realized through His Word that He dwells within us, for we our His temples. I read that greater is He who is inside of me than he who is in the world, for I am a son of God. I literally replaced my fears by believing what His Word says. If I have faith in God's Word, then Satan and sickness have no dominion over me and I shall not be afraid.

Sickness—A Result of Adam and Eve's Sin

If sickness and disease have no dominion over us, then why is sickness even here? Sickness is a direct result of the original sin. That sin is the sin of disobedience committed by Adam and Eve. From it the consequences of sickness and death were passed down to all humanity since Adam was considered to be the head of the whole human race.

Thus when Adam and Eve submitted to the temptation of the devil in the garden, they opened a floodgate of sin and sickness upon mankind. The second Adam, Jesus Christ, came to deliver you and me from the consequences of the first Adam's actions through His death and sufferings. If you will take all your sickness to the second Adam who is without sin, you are entitled to deliverance from your sicknesses just as you are from your sins.

You have a divine right to claim and walk in perfect health. A host of angels encamps around those who fear God, the Scriptures say. Because of what Jesus did, you have in your hands keys to the kingdom and keys to the king's treasury. It was because of Jesus' *act of faith* that you are now free. Adam's one *act* brought about sickness and disease. Jesus' one *act* brought about freedom from sickness, poverty, and death.

And not as it was by one that sinned, so is the gift: for the judgment was by one to condemnation, but the free gift is of many offences unto justification. For if by one man's offence death reigned by one; much more they which receive abundance of grace and of the gift of righteousness shall reign in life by one, Jesus Christ. Therefore as by the offence of one judgment came upon all men to condemnation; even so by the righteousness of one the free gift came upon all men unto justification of life. For as by one man's disobedience many were made sin-ners, so by the obedience of one shall many be made righteous. Moreover the law entered, that the offence might abound. But where sin abounded, grace did much more abound: that as sin hath reigned unto death, even so might grace reign through righteousness unto eternal life by Jesus Christ our Lord (Romans 5:16-21).

Chapter Four

Praise God Now for Your Healing!

Let every thing that hath breath praise the LORD.
Praise ye the LORD (Psalm 150:6).

You can use your mouth for many things. For instance, you can use it to eat with. You can use your tongue to speak with. Through your mouth you can breathe freely. But did you realize that God equipped you with a mouth primarily for you to praise Him? Your mouth and every part of your entire body were purposely designed by God to praise Him.

I always thought if people talked about me as much as they talk about the devil, I'd probably show up at every service just to hear what they were saying. Maybe that is the reason the devil shows up at church and in people's lives so frequently. Many believers spend more time praising the devil than they do glorifying God. You say, "Brother Coe, you've gone too far now. I do not give praises to the devil. You've got it all wrong, sir." Perhaps you just aren't recognizing it, but you are.

Listen, if you continually confess what the devil is doing and how he is making progress against your health, your family, and your finances, then you are giving him praise for what he does best. You are acknowledging and commending him on his work. You know that it is Satan's job to steal, kill, and destroy. So when he steals, kills, and destroys, why bother saying anything about it? You ought to confuse the enemy when he comes to interrupt your life instead of commenting on what he does.

You ask, "How can I confuse the devil?" All you have to do is begin to praise God in spite of whatever negative thing happens to you. That will confuse the devil so badly that he will be inclined to leave you alone after a while. Most Christians will readily praise God when things are going smoothly. They'll praise God when they get a new job, a new car, an increase in their wages, or a brand-new home. They'll praise God seemingly non-stop then.

But will you praise God when you've lost it all? How about if you found out that your entire family were just killed like Job's family was, would you praise the Lord right then and there? What if you discovered that your best friend just betrayed you without a justifiable cause? Could you praise Him then? It's easy to praise God when everything is going well. The real test comes when things are going badly, when your plans have all folded.

Praising God during those times is what confuses the enemy because he's the one bringing the bad times to you. And when you praise God in spite of how things are going, it makes the devil search out another person who will become so easily discouraged that he or she will use his or her tongue to give a voice to his or her pain. The devil likes to afflict people who will give him applause, not God.

People who use their tongues to praise and acknowledge the devil for his work are not just limited to the people who sit in the pews. Preachers fail this test time and time again. I've heard preachers say, "I feel like the devil has bound the service. He is hindering our progress." If you really think about it, this can't be true in God's service. If the devil's power were hindering me, I would shake it off through faith in God. The devil cannot bind a Spirit-filled saint if he or she will resist him.

The devil likes to afflict people who give him praise.

If a Christian permits him or herself to be bound, it is only because that believer does not recognize who he or she is and how much authority he or she has. In most cases when preachers say things like this, it is because they are just tired in their body. That person has wasted time during the day and failed to pray and read the Word. As a result, his or her mind was not focused on God. Now, in a weakened state, he or she feels really vulnerable to the devil.

Satan may have power, but he doesn't have that much power. In fact, the magnitude of his power is really controlled by us. In other words, we give the devil his daily allowance. Parents at times give their children a weekly allowance. Their allowance is solely based on whether or not they performed their duties in a satisfactory manner during the week. If the children performed well, they'd get their allowance and a possible bonus based on how their parents felt at that time.

If the children performed less than pleasing, then their parents may not give them anything. This is the same way that you should think when it comes to the devil. Don't give the devil any allowance. Starve him! He never does a good job. He is always doing mischievous and evil acts toward us. Therefore, he never deserves anything. In all things give God praise, glory, and thanks. When you start doing that and it becomes a regular habit, you will begin to understand how praise can precede your healing.

I will bless the LORD at all times: his praise shall continually be in my mouth (Psalm 34:1).

Why Does God Want Healthy Children?

Beloved, I wish above all things that thou mayest prosper and be in health, even as thy soul prospereth (3 John 2).

The Bible says that God wishes above all things that His children prosper and be in good health. God always knew that true wealth is good health. You can have all the money in the world, but if you are sick you can't enjoy it. What good is having ten million dollars, a 40-foot yacht, a ten million-dollar mansion, and a villa in the Caribbean, yet be confined to a hospital bed 24 hours a day? Money is only beneficial when you can use it to bless others and to support you and your family. Aside from that, merely having money is a useless pursuit if it cannot be utilized.

God is trying to get the message across that He wants His children to prosper. Your prosperity in every area of your life will be directly linked to how your soul prospers. Your mind has to continually be renewed by the Word of God in order for you to experience true prosperity. This is God's deepest desire for you. Unfortunately, so few actually live their lives at this level of God's expectancy. Most folks settle for just barely getting by in life. Most people say, "Well, I feel better than I did yesterday, so I guess that's better than nothing." God, on the other hand, says you ought to always be 100 percent, not every now and then.

Does God want you to be healthy for no reason, or is there a specific reason He wants you to prosper in your health? You must realize that God created you to praise Him. The very reason you exist is not to work a job and then retire. You are not here to save money and buy a nice home, educate your children in the finest schools, and join the Rotary Club. That's not why God created you. He created you for His glory!

All throughout the Psalms we see a consistent pattern of how God's name is to be praised. The Word commands us to *praise the Lord*. It goes on to tell us how *the name of the Lord* is the greatest, and how *the name of the Lord* is worthy of honor and glory. The only way that you can do that most effectively is if you are well and walking in divine health.

> *Let them praise the name of the LORD: for he commanded, and they were created* (Psalm 148:5).

Each one of your body parts performs a specific function. Your mouth opens and closes shut. Your voice box makes an audible sound and can speak. Each one of your hands has fingers that can move and grasp things. Both of your arms can lift your hands high in the air. Whether you walk or not depends on the condition of your feet and legs. Through your eyes you can see all of God's beautiful creations in the world. Even your neck has the ability to control the movement of your head.

Here's the good part. Each one of your body parts was created to give God praise. If your body parts are not working at their best, then they won't be able to give God the highest praise. You see, God never intended for your body to get sick in the first place. As we talked about earlier, Adam and Eve's disobedience caused this whole confusion. It was God's original plan that you and I would have perfectly whole bodies so that we could praise Him uninterrupted and unhindered.

When sickness came about, it deterred God's original plan. However, it did not cancel God's plan. Because of Jesus and the blood that He shed on Calvary's cross, we can once again reclaim divine health. And you don't have to settle for body parts that cannot be fully used for His glory. You don't have to tolerate being sick all the time as if that's normal. He wants all of you well, not just part of you or a part of the time.

God is so magnificent and glorious that we really do need all that He has given us to praise Him. Everything that is within us from our kidneys to our heart to our spleen was created to praise Him. It's the reason we are here. Once we accept that as truth, we will know for sure why God wants us healthy—to do His will.

Bless the LORD, O my soul; and all that is within me, bless His holy name! (Psalm 103:1 NKJV).

Prayer & Praise

Come and hear, all ye that fear God, and I will declare what he hath done for my soul. I cried unto him with my mouth, and he was extolled with my tongue. If I regard iniquity in my heart, the Lord will not hear me: but verily God hath heard me; he hath attended to the voice of my prayer. Blessed be God, which hath not turned away my prayer, nor his mercy from me (Psalm 66:16-20).

God's wants to show you how to pray. He desires to teach you how to pray. *"And it came to pass, that, as he was praying in a certain place, when he ceased, one of his disciples said unto him, Lord, teach us to pray, as John also taught his disciples"* (Luke 11:1). The reason

Jesus needed to teach His disciples how to pray is what they thought prayer was, really did not qualify as genuine prayer before God. So Jesus had to show them by His example and model how prayer should be practiced.

If you are going to pray to receive results, one of the first things you have to do is tear up your prayer list. You know—the prayer list that's a mile long asking God to gimme, gimme, gimme. And once God gives you what you have been asking for, He won't hear from you anymore until you want something else from Him. If you think that's prayer, you haven't really prayed.

Our prayers should be primarily praise.

Many people, possibly even including you, have been praying for God to do something for more than 15 years and haven't seen the answer yet. Because of that you got discouraged. I am here to tell you that if you will begin to pray through and combine your prayer with a heartfelt praise for God, He will tell you what to pray for. He also will tell you how to pray for it. It is at this point that you will receive everything that you ask for.

You might be thinking, *Brother Coe, you must be teaching that people shouldn't pray.* I'm not advocating anything like that at all. The Bible says, *"And he spake a parable unto them to this end, that men ought always to pray, and not to faint"* (Luke 18:1). However, our prayers should be primarily praise. In other words, if in prayer we praise God in advance for what we are believing for Him to do for us or in our lives, then we will receive what we desire.

If you want God to save your wayward children, don't beg God to save them. Start praising God in your prayer as if it is already done and you will have what you are praising God about. Get out of the begging mode and into the praising mode. Stop asking God to give you more money, a husband, a wife, or a new car. Those things are really not that difficult to get. In fact, you really don't need God to get most material things.

If you want a new car, all you have to do is manage you money well enough and save for a decent down payment and you can get any car that you desire. If you desire more money, then you will need to sow more money. It's that simple. If you desire a husband, prepare yourself spiritually, emotionally, and physically and he will notice you. Stop whining and complaining about what you don't have, act as if you already have received it, and it will be yours.

> *For verily I say unto you, That whosoever shall say unto this mountain, Be thou removed, and be thou cast into the sea; and shall not doubt in his heart, but shall believe that those things which he saith shall come to pass; he shall have whatsoever he saith. Therefore I say unto you, What things soever ye desire, when ye pray, believe that ye receive them, and ye shall have them* (Mark 11:23-24).

The Bible says that you need to *"believe that ye receive."* You may ask, "But Brother Coe, how can I believe that I receive when I don't see what I believe for in front of me?" That's where praise comes into the picture.

When you praise God for what you cannot see, it (what you cannot see) becomes real. Your praise for what you do not have is actually faith in action. Every time you praise God for what will be, you are acting like you've already received it. God honors that kind of faith. The more you praise Him, the more He'll produce for you.

Instead of saying, "God, I can't pay my bills. My rent is due, and I just don't have enough money," say, "Lord, I thank You for providing me with the necessary finances to meet all my needs. You are the supplier of everything that I need and desire, and I thank You for it right now."

Instead of saying, "I am so sick, Lord, please heal my tired body," say, "I thank You right now, Father, for being the Healer that You are. I thank You for providing me with impeccable health. I thank You that my health is better than it has ever been, and it's only going to get better from this point on." When you begin to praise God for what you desire, your desires will no longer be desires but will become reality for you. Praise the Lord!

God Doesn't Make People Sick

Bless the LORD, O my soul, and forget not all his benefits: who forgiveth all thine iniquities; who healeth all thy diseases; who redeemeth thy life from destruction; who crowneth thee with lovingkindness and tender mercies; who satisfieth thy mouth with good things; so that thy youth is renewed like the eagle's (Psalm 103:2-5).

People don't praise God like they really should because they have been falsely taught about God's actions toward humanity. I've heard people say things like, "God's going to put sickness on you if you don't do what He wants you to do. He's going to make you sick, sister." Nothing could be further from the truth. God is not trying to get you sick. He's trying to get you well and keep you that way. I can prove my point.

First, God cannot give you what He does not possess. God is the epitome of health and life. Therefore, that is all that He has to give you—health and life. If you asked me for 25 million dollars and I did not have it, then how could I give it to you? Obviously, I could not. I can only give you what I have, nothing more and nothing less. So God cannot give you sickness because there is no sickness in Him to pass on to you.

God is trying to make you well, not sick!

Second, God does everything with an intent and motive. He does not do anything just because. He is a very intentional God. The Bible says, *"For God so loved the world, that he gave his only begotten Son, that whosoever believeth in him should not perish, but have everlasting life. For God sent not his Son into the world to condemn the world; but that the world through him might be saved"* (John 3:16-17). Even from these verses we can clearly see that when God gave His Son, He did not do so without a reason.

73

God gave His Son so that He could get a return on His investment. He gave His Son as an exchange for you and me to be able to afford eternal life. All you and I have to do is believe on the name of the Lord, and we will be saved. Jesus made eternal life affordable for us. That was God's intention. What could God's intention possibly be for putting sickness and disease on His children? There is no way in the world that any loving and kind father would afflict his child with a disease. To do so would be hateful and malicious. God would do no such thing either.

God is an investment-minded God. He does everything with the expectancy of gaining a great return on His investment. If God made you sick, what then would He reap from such an investment—death? You see, it does not make any sense. God is a God of life. That is what He desires to give since He realizes that life regenerates and produces more life. Recognize that God does not get any glory out of putting sickness on you. The devil is the one who brings sickness and disease, not God.

This brings me to my third point. God puts hedges around you to shelter you from sickness, not expose you to it. Do you remember when the devil told God that the only reason Job served and loved Him is that God protected him by putting a hedge around him? Let's look at that passage in the Bible.

Hast not thou made an hedge about him, and about his house, and about all that he hath on every side? thou hast blessed the work of his hands, and his substance is increased in the land (Job 1:10).

God puts hedges of protection around His children so that Satan cannot have access to them. There are only two ways that God removes His hedge. The first is by a consensual agreement, as in the case of Job. God knew that by allowing the enemy to afflict Job that He would prove to the enemy that He had a servant who was rich in character, loyalty, and endurance. When these types of cases come to you, consider it an honor that God believes in you so strongly that He actually recommended for you to take a test that He already knew you would pass with flying colors.

The other way that God's hedge is removed is really not as much on Him as it is on us. When we violate covenant and when we give ourselves over to the spirit of betrayal without even realizing it, we reposition ourselves outside of God's divine will and thus outside of His protection. This is a dangerous place to be in since Satan then has free access to beat you literally to death. This is an area where so many people get confused.

You may see somebody sick and diseased and automatically assume that God has abandoned that person. This is most people's initial response. However, it is very possible that the person has abandoned God, not vice versa. God is not in the business of abandoning anyone. He is in the business of recruiting people who will love Him so much that they will praise Him continually. If God makes people sick, it would totally cancel His plan for creating man.

Before we continue, let's review the three points for your understanding:

God Doesn't Make People Sick Because...

1. God doesn't have sickness to give.

2. God is a wise investor. He only invests in what He can reap a fruitful return from. Sickness is contrary to His motive.

3. God puts hedges around you to shelter you from sickness.

Chapter Five

Focus Not on Man's Wisdom

━━

And when the sabbath day was come, he began to teach in the synagogue: and many hearing him were astonished, saying, From whence hath this man these things? and what wisdom is this which is given unto him, that even such mighty works are wrought by his hands? (Mark 6:2).

There is an area that I would like to deal with to clarify the truth that will make you free. God chooses and uses whomever He desires to accomplish His purposes on this earth. What I've just said was a loaded statement, and I don't want you to miss it. That means God does not need your vote or opinion on whether or not He should have chosen someone you believe He should not have.

God never chooses the noble and mighty, but rather the base things to demonstrate His glory in the earth.

The problem is that people within our modern-day society want us to qualify people by their standards, not God's. Therefore, they tend to focus more heavily on man's wisdom and not God's. Almost always they get into great confusion for doing so. You see, if you want to find out whether a doctor is a good doctor or not, you would more than likely be inclined to ask him or her for some credentials. You'd probably want to know what university the doctor attended, what kind of grades and honors he or she earned, and where he or she was a resident student.

After finding out those things, you would probably want to know how many people he or she has operated on. You'd want to know how successful these operations were. You might just ask if he or she had a list of referrals that you could call to do some background check information on them. For that profession, education is key to performing duties. But when it comes to working miracles, it is a totally different area that requires a different kind of training.

In Mark 6:2, the people in Jesus' times had a problem with understanding just how Jesus could perform the mighty works that He performed. After they heard Him preach and teach, they were absolutely astounded. They began to ask each other, "Where did this knowledgeable man come from? What great teacher did He study under? He must have been educated at the greatest schools to be able to teach and preach and perform miracles."

Little did they know that Jesus never sat at the feet of any great teacher; He was born in a manager among animals. His teacher was God. It was God who had anointed Him with the oil of wisdom above all His companions. It was only by the power that God gave Him that He could do the miracles that He did.

Although many people in Jesus' time did embrace His message, many others did not receive the message because they focused on His wisdom and had a difficult time validating its source. Since they felt Jesus did not have the correct credentials, they did not believe that He should perform miracles or even that the miracles that He did perform were actually God-sent. They had improper focus. Their improper focus caused them not to receive their healing. If you have improper focus, it'll cause you to miss out on your healing also.

Training for the Healing Ministry?

A man once came and questioned me, asking, "When God calls men into the healing ministry, why doesn't He call men with educations? Why doesn't He call our greatest college professors, skilled in the sciences, instead of unlearned men like W.V. Grant and William Branham, who never attended college?" After that he looked at me and probably felt it would be unfair to not include me in the direct interrogation. He asked, "Why did God even call you, an uneducated ex-soldier?" I really wish I knew the answer to that question.

One possible reason I believe God chooses people like Grant, Branham, and myself is that God knows we know our insufficiencies and failures. He realizes that none of us have any human qualities on which we can rely. Personally, I have never been trained to preach. I have no oratorical ability. I don't have degrees to help me in my ministry. Because of all the things that I don't have, I have to depend more than anyone else on the power of God. I have no other choice but to depend on God.

God chooses those who depend on Him.

There is no course that I can take that will adequately train me for every situation that will come up in the ministry. God uses different methods and ways of healing. Often He uses means that are totally strange to man's thinking. Thus I can't be limited to a manual on healing. I have to be open to what God is telling me for that particular moment—and that can change. So the training I need is called being sensitive to the Holy Spirit and hearing the voice of God.

Now, I am not discounting education. I believe that education has its rightful place. But when it comes to the supernatural and walking by faith, those are things God will have to teach you Himself. You can be trained to preach. You can be trained to write or even interpret the Word of God. But can you really be trained by men to be anointed? The only One who is qualified to teach that class is the One who anoints: the Lord Jesus Christ.

Would I be more or less qualified if I had earned a degree in divine healing? Would that make me a greater preacher and healer? It is quite possible that because of what I think I know I might have the propensity to become lifted up in pride. I could say, "Since I have this or that degree or this or that education, I really don't need God's oil on my life. All I need is the approval of an institution."

It is this spirit of pride that God vehemently rejects. Some people believe that because they are learned, they have nothing else to learn. They believe that since they have some knowledge, they have no need to seek out knowledge. As a result, God can't use them. So then God chooses to find someone who doesn't think he or she knows everything to work through. He knows that I know that when the miracle has been performed, He won't share the glory with any man. I know better than that. God and God only will get all the glory!

Jesus Still Heals the Blind and Causes the Lame to Walk

I was recently in a healing campaign in Oklahoma City, Oklahoma. In that meeting there was a blind man sitting right next to the platform where I was preaching. Directly behind him was a woman lying on a stretcher. When I noticed them, I came down off the platform and walked over to them. I asked the blind man, "Friend, how long have you been blind?" He responded, "Twenty-seven years."

I then asked the man, "Do you want to see?" What you must understand is that since this man could not see with his eyes, his focus could not be on me. It had to stay focused on Jesus. I knew this by his response. He answered, "Of course I do, Brother Coe." He said, "I believe God can cause me to see!" One of the preachers standing nearby said, "It will be a real miracle if that man sees. I doubt if that man even has eyeballs."

I had perceived in my spirit that this man had released faith for his healing. At that point, I laid my hands on the man. God instantly healed him, giving him perfect eyesight. Right in front of the crowd this man began counting how many fingers I held up. He followed me as I tiptoed around the tent. He was even able to identify certain things that I held up. The preacher who made the comment was totally amazed at what the Lord did.

There was a woman who attended my revival in Philadelphia, Pennsylvania, last summer. She was a member of a well-known denomination that never taught on divine healing. I believe her church may have even taught that the days of miracles were over. She came into the Metropolitan Opera House one evening and witnessed 27 persons being delivered from their crutches while they were standing in the prayer line. It was a glorious sight.

After she witnessed the mass miracles, she said, "Lord, I don't even have to walk up there. I know that You are an all-powerful God who can heal me right where I am." She lifted her hands toward heaven, and the Lord reached down and touched her right where she was. She wasn't focusing on man's wisdom but on the power of God. No matter where you are, you can always touch Jesus. When you pray, believe that you receive, and you shall have whatever you say.

Therefore I say unto you, What things soever ye desire, when ye pray, believe that ye receive them, and ye shall have them (Mark 11:24).

They Even Questioned Jesus

If you find it difficult to believe that people will judge your relationship with God, consider this: They even questioned Jesus.

Is not this the carpenter, the son of Mary, the brother of James, and Joses, and of Juda, and Simon? and are not his sisters here with us? And they were offended at him. But Jesus said unto them, A prophet is not without honour, but in his own country, and among his own kin, and in his own house. And he could there do no mighty work, save that he laid his hands upon a few sick folk, and healed them (Mark 6:3-5).

The people in the town felt as if Jesus could not teach them because they knew who He was. They may have known who He was, but they did not know whose He was. They did not realize to whom He belonged. That made all the difference in the world. It's not about who Jack Coe is. It is about to whom I belong. That's the right focus. I belong to Jesus. Some of you have said, "Isn't that Jack Coe, the fellow who was a soldier in the army?"

Yes, indeed, "I'm Jack Coe, the ex-solider." I'm not in Uncles Sam's army any longer, but I am in the army of the Lord and He has given me the power of the Holy Sprit

83

to cast off demons and heal the sick. It's not what we are but whom we serve that makes all the difference in the world. Because I serve a risen Savior, He covers me in areas where I am weak and empowers me by His Holy Spirit. Because I am in Christ, the things that would otherwise be unattainable for me are very possible. Don't look on man; look to Jesus.

> *Not that I speak in respect of want: for I have learned, in whatsoever state I am, therewith to be content. I know both how to be abased, and I know how to abound: every where and in all things I am instructed both to be full and to be hungry, both to abound and to suffer need. **I can do all things through Christ** which strengtheneth me* (Philippians 4:11-13).

Opening Up Your Heart to Jesus

✛═══✛

*And their eyes were opened, and they knew him;
and he vanished out of their sight. And they said
one to another, Did not our heart burn within us,
while he talked with us by the way, and while he
opened to us the scriptures? (Luke 24:31-32).*

It is a most wonderful experience when your heart burns
within you. Some people don't know what that actually means. Allow me to explain this experience. Jesus
had long prophesied to His disciples that He was going
to die and that in three days He would be resurrected.
Some believed Him. Many others did not. Of those who
did believe Him was a company of dedicated women
who followed Jesus closely during His earthly ministry.

It is unfortunate that the very ones who did not believe are the very ones who should have believed the words of Jesus—His own disciples. Surely as Jesus had prophesied, He was crucified, buried, and arose on the third day. The Holy Scripture records the words that Jesus spoke: *"...The Son of man must be delivered into the hands of sinful men, and be crucified, and the third day rise again"* (Luke 24:7). On the third day, the day Jesus predicted He would be resurrected, this company of women and others went to visit Jesus' tomb to see whether or not He actually had risen.

To their amazement, when they arrived at the tomb the stone that covered the entrance was rolled away. Jesus was not there. His linen wrapping was the only thing there. Yet, it appeared that Jesus was missing. All those who sincerely loved the Lord were obviously sorrowful after hearing the saddening news. Not only had Jesus died and left them, but now His bodily remains were also missing.

The very same day two of the disciples were returning home to Emmaus, which was about a seven-mile walk from Jerusalem. During their walk they were talking about Jesus and all the events that had recently happened around His death and sudden disappearance. While they were walking and talking, Jesus appeared and began to walk with them. They did not realize that it was Jesus, however.

Interrupting their probing conversation, Jesus asked them, "What is it that you brothers are talking so deeply about?" The two disciples were totally surprised by the lack of knowledge this Stranger showed. The crucifixion of Jesus and the prophecy concerning His rising up was the talk of the town. There was not a soul living within those regions who had not heard of what was going on. So they thought it was quite odd that this Man did not know about the breaking news. They assumed that He must not have been from those parts. Certainly He must have been a stranger.

After listening to their concerns, their doubts, their disbeliefs, and the things they were unclear about, Jesus responded to them. He accused both men of being foolish. Jesus could not understand why it was so hard for them to believe the prophecies that were given about the Messiah. These prophecies were written in the Scriptures and the followers of Jesus were mainly converted Jews who knew the Scriptures very well.

Jesus began to quote several scriptures beginning with Moses and continuing to all the Prophets pertaining to the coming Messiah. By this time it was late and they had reached their destination, but Jesus had a further distance to travel. Very much enthused by their conversation with Jesus and being genuinely hospitable, they insisted that Jesus stay the night with them. Jesus agreed.

When they ate dinner, Jesus, as it was His tradition, asked the Father's blessing over the food. Suddenly it hit them. They realized whom they had been talking and fellowshipping with all along. They knew through communion with Jesus exactly who He was. Both men agreed that they experienced a feeling that literally felt like their hearts were burning while they talked to Jesus. Their hearts burned with the beautiful warmth of being

87

so intimately connected to the living Word. At first they did not know whom they were with. They only came to the realization after they had opened their hearts.

Lord, I Am Wide Open to You

What does it mean to be wide open to God? Being wide open to God means that God has free access to your mind and spirit. When you are wide open to God, He does not need to ask special permission to enter your life. You've already given Him an open invitation to move freely through you. In the area of your mind, God has total freedom to influence your thoughts to become like His thoughts. And your openness to that process makes you vulnerable to Him and teachable in His presence.

The opposite of being open is obviously being closed to the things of God. It is being closed to what God is doing in the here and now. People who fit this category often say things like, "That's not the way God did it before, so I am pretty certain that He's not doing it that way now. If that were really a move of God, I would have seen it before. I've never seen that in the Bible before." When you hear people utter phrases like those, you can automatically conclude that they are not open to the Spirit of God.

The way God did things before are not necessarily how God will do them today. And that's completely all right. It's not a bad thing. My openness to God gives Him the allowance to be God in my life, in my thoughts, and over all my affairs. Notice I did not say that my openness to God gives Him the allowance to be God. God will be God whether or not I approve of Him or give Him allowance. He doesn't need my vote to be God. He was God long before I was born, and He will be God long after I am gone from this earth.

However, you have to *allow* God to work and move about freely in your life. If He is going to spiritually impact you, you have to give Him the freedom to do so. God has to feel welcomed in your life. If He doesn't, then He will neither stay nor will He have the right kind of atmosphere to heal you.

Your openness allows God to be God in your life.

Most people close God out when they are unfamiliar with His methods. One thing I would like to make clear to you is that God will use various methods to heal His people. Very often the methods that He uses will be totally strange to your natural mind. However, if you are wide open, it really won't matter how He chooses to heal. His healing you is all that will matter.

Some years ago in Springfield, Missouri, a woman had traveled more than 200 miles by car to attend my revival service. The ushers seated her on the very first row. This woman was dying of a terminal form of cancer. While she was sitting there, she was intently listening to me talk about the goodness of the Lord Jesus Christ and what He could do if only you would be open to Him.

While I was preaching, her faith was increasing, and God began to renew her strength. I felt impressed by the

Lord to begin reading the Holy Word aloud. I began to read scriptures about people in the Bible who were lying at the point of death yet were miraculously healed by the power of God. All of a sudden this woman began to say after each verse I read, "Lord, that's Thy Word." She kept on saying this until it began to burn within her heart. She began to feel the presence of God so strongly that she knew that Jesus was right there with her on the front row.

She stretched forth her hand and said these words, "Lord, if what he is preaching is true, and I know that it is because it's the Word of God, I am going to stretch forth my hand and believe that You will take the cancer out of my body." When she did this, the Lord stretched His hand toward her and the cancer literally disappeared. She jumped up and began praising the Lord with a loud voice. Right during the middle of my message she jumped up and said, "Brother Coe, I am healed! God has taken the cancer out of my body—it's gone!"

I had never physically touched this woman. That did not matter. The touch that she needed most was the touch of the Lord, not mine. But it was when she opened herself wide to what God was doing and began to apply the Word of God to her situation that God actually healed her. Her personal prejudices and dislikes could have caused her to miss out on her healing. But she chose to be open-minded. Your prayer too should be, "Lord, any way You bless me or heal me, I will be satisfied. If it's not the way that I believe it should be, it really won't matter as long as it is the way You want it to be, in Jesus' name."

The Power of the Burning Word in Scripture

There are many places in the Scriptures where the power of the burning word is revealed. A better way of looking at and understanding the burning word is to think of it as God revealing Himself through the Word. Yet another angle is to look at it as the manifested presence of God's Word with us and in us. It is the power of hearing and receiving God's Word that brings about healing in our bodies. The Word heals. And once we receive the Word through willingness in our spirit to be wide open, then and only then can the Word produce results in the life of the believer.

Although I could have listed far more than I did, following are five scriptures from the Bible that help to clarify my point that God's Word burning within us will always produce favorable results in our life. I've added some brief commentary on each of the scriptures listed. I hope that you will find these and my comments not only encouraging but also as scriptural evidence on how effective the living Word actually is.

1. *"I rejoice at thy word, as one that findeth great spoil"* (Psalm 119:162).

I get excited about God's Word in the same way a person rejoices when he or she finds millions of dollars. His Word is greater than riches.

2. *"And Simon answering said unto him, Master, we have toiled all the night, and have taken nothing: nevertheless at thy word I will let down the net"* (Luke 5:5).

91

Peter had been working all night long trying to catch fish. He caught nothing. Jesus spoke His words over Peter's situation. He told Peter to let down his nets for a big catch of fish. Peter knew that Jesus was not a fisherman by trade. He thought perhaps Jesus did not understand that if the fish were not biting all night long, it was probably not a good time for fishing. But the Bible says Peter took Jesus at His word. Hearing and acting on the Word of God in Peter's heart caused him to catch the greatest amount of fish that he ever caught in his life.

3. *"This is my comfort in my affliction: for thy word hath quickened me"* (Psalm 119:50).

Not only does God's Word preserve my life, but it also literally gives me life. I take comfort in knowing that.

4. *"He sent his word, and healed them, and delivered them from their destructions"* (Psalm 107:20).

If I don't preach a four-point message, dot all of my i's and cross all of my t's, that is fine. As long as I read the Word of God, simply hearing God's Word will heal people. I've seen it happen hundreds of times. God will instruct me not to preach or even to do a whole lot of singing. He will tell me to just read the Word. He won't necessarily direct me to a scripture that deals directly with healing. It could be about a varied number of things mentioned in the Bible. But the very reading of His Word amazingly heals people of their diseases. I believe God chooses to tell me to do this from time to time because He wants me to stay in the full knowledge of who is actually performing the healing. I'm not healing anybody. It's His Word that heals.

5. *"The centurion answered and said, Lord, I am not worthy that thou shouldest come under my roof: but speak the word only, and my servant shall be healed"* (Matthew 8:8).

A centurion had a servant who was sick unto death and needed Jesus' healing power to heal him. However, since the commanding soldier was a man in authority, he understood the authority and power of words. He commanded army troops to go here and there, and they did so based on the authority of their commanding officer's word. Knowing that the power in Jesus' words was far greater than any other person's word, he asked Jesus to simply speak words of healing. He felt that it would not be necessary to ask Jesus to come into his house. He respected Jesus' time. He told the Lord, *"speak the word only."* That means, don't do anything else. The Word is the only needed thing now. Jesus was amazed at how strong this man's faith was. Immediately his servant was healed. Was he healed by Jesus' personal visitation or touch? No, the *word* healed him.

If you make it your goal to begin to believe God's Word from now on, His Word will produce amazing results in your life too.

Rejecting the Word Is Rejecting Jesus

He that rejecteth me, and receiveth not my words, hath one that judgeth him: the word that I have spoken, the same shall judge him in the last day (John 12:48).

In the beginning was the Word, and the Word was with God, and the Word was God (John 1:1).

God and His Word are one. It is impossible to separate Jesus Christ from the words that He spoke or from the Word that God inspired men to write about Him. So, what Jesus says is actually who He is. If Jesus speaks about healing, He can do so because He *is* healing. Healing is not what Jesus does as much as it is who He is.

Jesus said unto her, I am the resurrection, and the life: he that believeth in me, though he were dead, yet shall he live: and whosoever liveth and believeth in me shall never die. Believest thou this? (John 11:25-26).

Notice that in this scripture Jesus did not say that He gives life; He said He is the life. Jesus' words are equal in strength and delivering power to Himself. Once you begin to believe and receive and act on His words, then you will start to experience the glory of God in your life. But when you reject His words, you are actually rejecting Jesus. You have closed off your heart to what He is saying and, more importantly, to what He desires to do in your life.

From this point on, you must begin to accept both Jesus and His words. To reject either is equal to rejecting God. And on judgment day God will hold you accountable for rejecting Him. He takes this very personally. Just imagine on judgment day, God says to you, "I am bringing a judgment against you." You ask God, "What have I done wrong, Lord? I have lived a holy life as closely to the Bible as I could. I didn't chase women; I did not smoke cigarettes or drink booze, and I attended church every time the doors were open. Lord, I lived the best way that I could."

Then God says, "True, you have done all those things. But you did not receive My Word. I told you in My Word that healing belonged to you, yet you chose to remain sick and diseased. That greatly disappointed Me." Wouldn't it feel totally horrible to be judged because you closed yourself off to the truth of His Word? God's Word is designed for your total benefit. It was created as a manual for you to experience an abundant life. If you choose not to seize the good life that God has made possible through His Word, you are only robbing yourself of God's best. Worse than that, you are rejecting God at the same time.

To reject the Word is to reject God.

Christ Makes My Heart Burn Within

Every time Jesus walks with me, my heart burns within me. I have been discouraged and almost defeated at times in my life. Whenever this dreadful feeling comes over me, I quickly turn to Jesus and His Word. In my darkest and loneliest hour He begins to walk right beside me. And when He does, He causes my heart to feel so warmed. My spirit instantly becomes encouraged and lifted up.

But thou, O LORD, art a shield for me; my glory, and the lifter up of mine head. I cried unto the LORD with my voice, and he heard me out of his holy hill. Selah (Psalm 3:3-4).

95

There is an old hymn that I was singing in Hutchinson, Kansas, called "In the Garden." When we got to the part of the song that says, "He walks with me and he talks with me," I began to feel this burning in my heart. I knew that Jesus was right there in our midst. I told the people, "Right now you can feel the hand of Jesus. Just stretch out your hand." When everyone began to stretch forth their hands, God began to move by His power.

A woman who had been agonizing with pain throughout the entire service was healed by the power of God. She explained that as she stretched her hand forward, she could not see her hand at all. She felt a burning sensation in her hand and that burning went up her arm, but she could not physically see her hand. What she did see was another hand that seemed to cover her hand, wrist, and part of her lower arm. She couldn't help but recognize that the hand covering hers had a nail print.

It was then that she became fully aware that it was the hand of Jesus that was touching her hand. She asked the Lord, "Lord, do You really love me that much? Do You really care enough about me to come down and place Your hand on mine?" Her experience does not have to be an isolated one. You too can feel your heart burn within you simply by opening your spirit to His Word. When you do, your life will never be the same.

Chapter Seven

God Usually Uses Foolish Things

+=====+

But God hath chosen the foolish things of the world to confound the wise; and God hath chosen the weak things of the world to confound the things which are mighty; and base things of the world, and things which are despised, hath God chosen, yea, and things which are not, to bring to nought things that are: that no flesh should glory in his presence (1 Corinthians 1:27-29).

God often uses foolish things, or foolish methods, to bring about healing. I don't always understand His methods; I just do what He says and expect the best. He never fails to honor His Word. But the things that He often asks me to do are so ridiculous that I can understand why so many people question the things that I do.

If I did not flow in the supernatural I would not understand why God does the things that He does either. In order to begin to understand God's reasoning, you must first be born again and filled with the Holy Ghost.

Why is that? If you are not filled with the Holy Ghost, you definitely will not be sensitive to what the Spirit of God is saying. You will rather be prone to do what people expect you to do. The problem with that is, if you want to be greatly used by God, you have to rid yourself of the opinions of men. Your value system has to change completely. When you prioritize, God and His Word have to be at the top of your list. Man and his opinion should be far below on that list.

God Used Me to Do Foolish Things

I was preaching at a church in Dallas, Texas, and the wife of the pastor of that church came into my healing line for prayer. This woman was very beautiful in her appearance. She dressed very dignified, she looked her best, and one could tell from looking at her that she had it all together. The Lord spoke to me and said, "Take a handful of olive oil, put it on your hands, then slap her in the face with it." I thought that it would be completely foolish to do such a thing.

However, I knew that it was also completely God to do such a thing. So when she came up to me, I smeared oil all over her face and then slapped her. She fell on the floor and began to roll back and forth in the dust. This dignified woman was losing all of her dignity. Yet, when she arose to her feet, she was completely healed by the power of God. It was foolish, but it worked.

Someone recently asked me, "Where does Brother Oral Roberts get that laying hands on the radio stuff? I've never seen that in the Bible before." First off, radios were not even in the Bible; neither was electricity. The laying on of hands, however, is in the Bible. And if God told Brother Roberts to tell people to lay their hands on the radio and receive their healing, then that is exactly what they should do. Thousands of people have come forward to testify how they received their healing when they did this by faith. It doesn't make sense to the natural mind, but it makes a whole lot of sense to God.

A number of church leaders were upset with me because I mailed out thousands of gold prayer cloths that I prayed over. The Lord told me to do it. Again, they said, "Brother Coe, that's not in the Bible. I've never seen a gold prayer cloth in the Bible." I said, "You have seen prayer cloths and handkerchiefs in the Bible, haven't you?" They all agreed. I said, "Then what difference does it make whether they are gold, purple, blue, black, or polka dot?"

I have received thousands upon thousands of letters to my office from people who have used these cloths by faith and were healed from cancer, tuberculosis, headaches, and other diseases. The method may have seemed a bit foolish. But it worked, and that is what matters most. If it were up to me, I would choose a far more sensible way of doing things. But I am not God.

And whatever way He chooses, regardless to how foolish it may seem, I am going to do it God's way. A long time ago, I settled in my spirit that I would much rather use God's foolish ways of doing things and get healed than use my intelligent ways of doing things and stay sick and die.

God Has Good Reasons for Using Foolish Things

That no flesh should glory in his presence (1 Corinthians 1:29).

There is one thing that I have learned about God: God won't share His glory with anyone. So God will often allow your situation to become so depleted that nothing short of a miracle will ever pull you through. He does this to ensure His investment and protect Himself. He does this to ensure that He will get all the glory after the healing has occurred or after the miracle has been wrought.

Man always tends to want to be praised and recognized before people. That by itself is not wrong. God does not have a problem with you being praised for your accomplishments. In fact, the Bible actually suggests that you give proper praise and honor to the people who deserve it. *"Render therefore to all their due: taxes to whom taxes are due, customs to whom customs, fear to whom fear, honor to whom honor"* (Romans 13:7 NKJV). The contention enters the moment you believe you are responsible for what God is doing.

It's very obvious that there are some things in life God is responsible for doing and other things you are responsible for doing. God is not going to tie your shoelaces. He won't literally feed you food with a spoon and a fork. God won't choose the clothes that you wear and assist you in getting dressed. He won't rear your children for you. Don't be confused about the matter at all. I promise you that God will give you the strength to do all those things, but He won't do them for you. You have to do those things yourself.

God won't share His glory with you.

However, there are some things that you cannot do. And God does not expect you to do them since He knows you don't have the capacity to get the job done. For example, if you have cancer in your body, you can't heal yourself. That's His job. Cancer is far too large for you to try to tackle on your own. If you do, it will kill you. You need God to battle against that awful disease for you. I've seen people try to combat cancer with their limited knowledge and strength, getting sicker by the minute.

Healing is God's gift to us, not our gift to Him. So when God heals you, you must be careful not to forget to give Him all the glory. Since God knows that we will have challenges in this area of giving Him the glory, He has set up a win-win situation for the believer. "Brother Coe, what do you mean?" What I mean is that God will use some of the most ridiculous methods to get His mission accomplished. He doesn't choose ridiculous methods because He wants a good laugh every now and then. He chooses these methods to safeguard your ego.

Think about it. If you punch a woman in the stomach as hard as you can—a woman who has full-blown colon cancer—if it's not God telling you to do that, you are going to be in some deep water. If God told you to do it, the foolish act will be exchanged for a rewarding victory. However, if you believed that you had the power to do this on your on, your foolish act will be exchanged for some silver handcuffs. You will go to jail for murder. This method of using foolish things is no new thing. God has been employing this method for a very long time.

Foolish Spitting

Then they brought to Him one who was deaf and had an impediment in his speech, and they begged Him to put His hand on him. And He took him aside from the multitude, and put His fingers in his ears, and He spat and touched his tongue. Then, looking up to heaven, He sighed, and said to him, "Ephphatha," that is, "Be opened." Immediately his ears were opened, and the impediment of his tongue was loosed, and he spoke plainly. Then He commanded them that they should tell no one; but the more He commanded them, the more widely they proclaimed it (Mark 7:32-36 NKJV).

Then He came to Bethsaida; and they brought a blind man to Him, and begged Him to touch him.

So He took the blind man by the hand and led him out of the town. And when He had spit on his eyes and put His hands on him, He asked him if he saw anything. And he looked up and said, "I see men like trees, walking." Then He put His hands on his eyes again and made him look up. And he was restored and saw everyone clearly (Mark 8:22-25 NKJV).

Foolish Washing

And many lepers were in Israel in the time of Elisha the prophet, and none of them was cleansed except Naaman the Syrian (Luke 4:27 NKJV).

Now Naaman, commander of the army of the king of Syria, was a great and honorable man in the eyes of his master, because by him the LORD had given victory to Syria. He was also a mighty man of valor, but a leper (2 Kings 5:1 NKJV).

And Elisha sent a messenger to him, saying, "Go and wash in the Jordan seven times, and your flesh shall be restored to you, and you shall be clean." But Naaman became furious, and went away and said, "Indeed, I said to myself, 'He will surely come out to me, and stand and call on the name of the LORD his God, and wave his hand over the place, and heal the leprosy.' Are not the Abanah and the Pharpar, the rivers of Damascus, better than all the waters of Israel? Could I not wash in them and be clean?" So he turned and went away in a rage (2 Kings 5:10-12 NKJV).

Feelings, Foolish Things, and Your Healing

Allow me to clarify one thing for you as it relates to feelings and your healing. It really does not matter what people feel when they are prayed for. Quite often people who receive their healing do not feel anything at all. The feeling does not matter; your faith does. When Jesus Christ sees the faith in your heart and He speaks His Word, you are guaranteed healing.

We live in such an emotional world. And there is nothing wrong with emotions. There is a time for being emotional. Often that time is in the house of God while worshipping in the presence of the Lord. Emotions are not evil. However, they do not have to be present in order for God to heal. God's healing is always based on one of two things: faith and His sovereign will.

I've seen ministers screaming at the top of their lungs in an effort to try to get someone healed. The person still died. According to God's Word, we the believers have authority over sickness and disease. All we have to do to get the devil to move out is to believe that we have the authority to evict him and then exercise that authority.

Nowhere in the Bible will you see a passage that says, "And Jesus yelled and healed them." That wasn't Jesus' style or approach. Jesus neither commanded people to stand on their heads nor shook them in order to get them healed. The Bible clearly explains how healing happened then and how it still happens until this very day.

> *He sent His word and healed them, and delivered them from their destructions. Oh, that men would give thanks to the LORD for His goodness, and for His wonderful works to the children of men!* (Psalm 107:20-21).

Jesus healed them by the Word. He raised Lazarus from the dead with His Word. He spoke words and demons departed. There is power in the words of Jesus. I am not denying that the manifestation of God's power will at times cause people to jerk and shiver. Those kinds of uncontrollable expressions happen very often. But you should not be confused by the emotional responses to God's power and the singularity of His power. There is a difference.

Your feeling does not matter; your faith does.

People and cultures all over the world respond totally differently to death, sickness, or even pleasure. Some will outwardly show and even demonstrate their pain. Others will hold it in and not show it at all. Those are two very different responses to the same feeling of pain. But there are some people who appear to be totally losing their minds when they feel the slightest sensation. The point is, the response does not lessen the measure of pain they are feeling.

Interestingly enough, not one place in the Scriptures do you see Jesus laying His hands upon a demon-possessed

105

person. We practice this method out of our tradition (and it is not necessarily a bad tradition). God looks on our hearts and sees our sincerity and extends His grace to us despite the methods we sometimes choose. So what about the foolish things? Understand that you do not have to make up a whole bunch of foolish deeds to try to get God's attention or the people's attention.

The bottom line is that if God tells you to do something, and if you *know* that it is God speaking and not just your imagination, then do it. When you operate with that kind of faith conviction, you are operating foolishly according to the world's way of thinking. True faith always goes against the established thinking of modern-day Pharisees. Even Jesus' using words to heal people and giving us, the believers, the authority to do the same is quite foolish.

How can mere words heal, or increase people financially, or even cause people to come to Christ? The method definitely makes the intellectual world wonder in amazement and often criticize. Nonetheless, the methods still work and they still get results regardless of how foolish you believe they are. Remember that the very nature of faith is foolish. We believe (have faith in) a God we cannot see. We talk to Him and hear Him talk to us, yet no one else can validate that we are actually hearing Him speak.

The doctor says you will die within the next three months, yet after two years you are still alive and doing better than ever. That's foolish to man's understanding. Your faith will never make practical, logical, reasonable sense—particularly to the carnally minded Christian or the worldly person. The good thing is that it really does not matter whether or not it makes sense; it still works.

Frequently Asked Questions About Healing

1. Why did God heal me of one thing, yet the other sickness that was in my body remained?

Although God has the power to heal you totally, your faith is still required to execute that healing. You may have believed God to heal the pain in your back, and He did. That does not automatically mean that He will heal your diabetes too. As I have said, He can do it, but He does not always do it. God takes great pleasure in healing you; however, often you don't receive total healing simply because you have not asked. You will receive your healing for an issue simply by asking *specifically* for it.

Ye ask, and receive not, because ye ask amiss, that ye may consume it upon your lusts (James 4:3).

2. I've been through several prayer lines and received prayer from anointed ministers. Why am I still not healed?

First, I want you to know that your persistence will be rewarded in due season. God honors your faithful pursuit of His healing promises. But what I don't want you to get confused about is this: God does not want you to limit your belief to thinking that only by seeking out anointed men and women of God will you get your healing.

Obviously, there is nothing at all wrong with going to crusades and healing revivals with an expectation of receiving your healing. However, if you believe the only way you can be healed is through this famous healing personality, you may very well short-circuit the power of God. God can use anyone He chooses to transmit His power through. He can use a little boy or girl, an old man or woman, your pastor, or a deacon at your ministry to pray the prayer of faith and you will be healed. God ultimately wants every believer to fully recognize that the power to heal belongs to Him and that if you look to Him for your healing, you will be healed regardless of what person or vehicle He chooses to use.

3. Is it God's will to heal everyone?

I've heard this question over and over again. This question is no different than asking, "Is it God's will for everyone to be saved?" The answer to that question is pretty obvious. He sincerely desires that everybody becomes born again. In fact, His Word says, *"The Lord is not slack concerning his promise, as some men count slackness; but is longsuffering to us-ward, not willing that any should perish, but that all should come to repentance"* (2 Peter 3:9). The Bible is very clear on the issue of salvation as well as of healing. It is God's will to heal everyone, yet everyone will not be healed.

A will is nothing more than a written document of someone's desires being carried out and his or her wealth and property being properly disbursed. Just because someone has a written will does not automatically mean that everyone who was a benefactor in the will, will actually receive what is his or hers. First the people whose names are written in the will must know that their names are in it. Then they have to know that they have a right to claim what is in it. They have to find where they need to go to get what is theirs. Then they have to claim their possessions. It is the same way with your healing. So many people don't even realize that their names are written in the will—the one that provides us with daily healing. Most Christians know about their names being written in the Lamb's Book of Life. But you can only cash in on that after you die. While you are here on earth, God has many blessings for you to enjoy and one of those blessings is divine healing. Healing is a choice. Whether you claim it or not is totally up to you. It's available for you, but it won't force itself upon you. You've got to stake your claim on it using God's Word to verify that you really do have a right to it.

4. Does God heal sinners?

God heals sinners all the time. Jesus did it in the New Testament and He still does it now. One of the main reasons God does this is to show His glory, power, and love to the unbeliever with the expectation of that unbeliever accepting the love of Christ into his or her life. Many times people who have been saved for a very long time can get caught up into their own pride and their own traditional belief system that often excludes the power of God working personally in their lives. Because it is the very nature of God to heal, He has to continuously heal people. So "whosoever" will be healed is who God is looking for, whether they are saved or not. Ultimately healing is the children's bread and belongs to believers. But if believers continue to forfeit what belongs to them, then it will go to others. Below are a few scriptures that bear witness to the truth that Jesus heals sinners, even the demon possessed.

And his fame went throughout all Syria: and they brought unto him all sick people that were taken with divers diseases and torments, and those which were possessed with devils, and those which were lunatic, and those that had the palsy; and he healed them (Matthew 4:24).

And he healed many that were sick of divers diseases, and cast out many devils; and suffered not the devils to speak, because they knew him (Mark 1:34).

5. If I fall out under the power of God, does that mean that I am healed?

No, not necessarily. There are people who fall out under the power who are not always healed. Sometimes they are and sometimes they are not. Falling under the power of God does not equal healing. The only thing that falling out under the power of God says is that your body has become overwhelmed and inundated by the power of God to the extent that you can no longer stand up. Your knees get weakened to the point that you fall into His arms and His presence. Often while you are "out under the power," healing takes place. But sometimes healing happens after that. Don't focus on whether or not you "fall out." Focus on your ability to tune into your healing. Being receptive to Him—more than any particular manifestation—will get you into the place where healing happens.

Chapter Eight

Don't Look at the Symptoms

What are symptoms? And exactly why shouldn't we look at symptoms? You may think, *I've always used symptoms as a barometer to measure my healing. If I am truly healed, then I won't have any symptoms. If I have any symptoms, then I surely couldn't be healed.*" Nothing could be further from the truth. And I'll prove it to you.

symptom

   1 a : subjective evidence of disease or physical disturbance; *broadly* : something that indicates the presence of bodily disorder **b:** an evident reaction by a plant to a pathogen

   2 a : something that indicates the existence of something else... **b** : a slight indication: trace.[1]

---

1. *Merriam-Webster's Collegiate Dictionary*, 10th edition (Springfield, Massachusetts: Merriam-Webster, Inc., 1996), "symptom."

Symptoms are used for two reasons. In the medical arena, they are used early on to detect a problem that could become fatal. That is a good thing. But you must understand that God's kingdom is not at all like the kingdom of this world. In the kingdom of God, symptoms

Having symptoms simply means you have to stand in faith.

arise to give rise to our faith. The believer never looks at symptoms as a determining factor to his or her healing. When symptoms arise, it only means that you have to stand in faith and continue to confess what you believe God said about your condition.

For we walk by faith, not by sight (2 Corinthians 5:7).

It's one thing to be healed, but it is a very different thing when you begin to thank and praise God long before the manifestation of your healing actually arrives. If you know in your heart that God has healed your body, then you should begin to thank Him for your healing right now, regardless of the symptoms that may still exist. The very act of your thanking God while symptoms exist is an act of faith, and in the process of your thanking God for your healing, the manifestation will happen. So whatever you do, don't look at the symptoms because they will not only confuse you but also will eventually distract you from receiving your intended goal—healing.

When I served in the United States Army, I contracted malaria. I can clearly remember when God healed me at 2:00 in the morning. Every day prior to my healing I would suffer quite badly from chills. Like clockwork they would come at 4:00 each afternoon. The very same day after God touched my body with His healing hand, as it was approaching the 4:00 hour, the devil spoke to me and said, "It's almost four o'clock now. It's time for your chills." I responded, "Yes it is, isn't it."

He said, "You're feeling those pains in the back of your neck right now, aren't you?" I said, "Let me see. Yes, I believe they are there. Yes, they are!" He said, "They're going down your spine right now. You're getting a headache and your temperature is rising," he insisted. In all reality I neither sensed a headache nor was I feeling feverish at all. But because I did not cast down the thoughts that the enemy was bringing to me, I began to believe that I was getting a fever and that I had a splitting headache.

I actually started to anticipate symptoms, even though they had not even arrived as yet. The whispers of the enemy, which I listened to, caused me to act on those symptoms that I was so accustomed to having. As a result, I did my normal routine of taking off my clothes and getting into bed underneath the covers, just waiting for the chills to begin and end as quickly as possible. Until God asked me, "Why are you in bed? What are you doing there?"

I answered, "I am waiting for the chills and fever to come." He said, "Didn't I heal you last night, or don't you remember?" He said, "Get up now, get your clothes on, and go down to the street corner and preach." Quite honestly I never really liked to preach on the street corner; it's never been my personal interest. But of course that did not matter since it wasn't about me but about Jesus. I did what God told me to do. I put my clothes on and started walking down the street to my assignment.

As I was walking, I could hear voices speaking to me trying to deter my progress. The enemy was trying to convince me on my short walk that I was going to have a major malaria attack and suddenly die right there on the street. Finally realizing the enemy's tactics, I simply refused to acknowledge in my mind anything that he was saying. I followed through on my orders and preached on the corner.

Three people were born again that day in Troup, Texas. Since that day, since that stand, I have never had another bout with malaria again. Because I took a stand and refused to acknowledge symptoms or acknowledge the enemy's voice, I received the manifestation of my healing. I learned that day "how to" resist the devil. Suddenly my eyes opened to the meaning of the scripture, *"Submit yourselves therefore to God. Resist the devil, and he will flee from you"* (James 4:7).

Although I was saved and filled with the Holy Ghost, I was still not totally submitted to God. What I mean by that is I was not submitted to what His Word said about my healing. When God said that I was healed, that should have been it, once and for all. I should have totally accepted my healing as a reality. But instead I allowed my symptoms, or the enemy's thoughts concerning them, to overrule what I knew was true.

Don't Look at the Symptoms

The enemy will always work in your life through your subconscious mind. He tries his best to wiggle his way into your mind to confuse you about what God's Word says. If you are truly submitted to God, then whatever He says about your life will be your reality, nothing less. And when that occurs, you can resist the devil and he will flee from you. But beware of symptoms, for symptoms will always compromise your faith.

Chapter Nine

Why Partial Healings?

There has been a whole lot of talk about partial healings these days. (We already touched on this subject briefly, but it bears repeating.) People ask, "Why does God heal me of one thing but leave something else, another kind of sickness, in my body?" The answer to that question is really quite simple. That is all you asked Him to heal you of. A person may be dying from a cancerous condition as well as suffer from arthritis in the feet and hands. Perhaps he or she deals with gallstones also.

To that person, the gallstones and arthritis are not as serious as the cancer since the cancer is more immediately life-threatening. He or she gets desperately serious with God and begins to cry out before Him, "God, if you don't heal this cancer, I am going to die. God, I am trusting in You. I am getting into that healing line. I want this cancer healed now."

Suddenly, when the person gets up there, the thing that is most dominant in his or her mind is the very thing that God does for that person. This individual has only one thing on his or her mind, and that is getting healed from cancer. Such a person is not thinking at all about the gallstones or arthritis. In fact, deep down within, he or she really believes that if he or she can just get the cancer healed, he or she has driven a pretty good bargain with God. What the person doesn't realize is that God wants to heal him or her from *all* sickness and disease. It is not until way later, after receiving healing from cancer, that the person recognizes that he or she needs to be healed from other things. So why didn't that person get healed from the other things? The answer remains the same. He or she did not ask.

> *Ye lust, and have not: ye kill, and desire to have, and cannot obtain: ye fight and war, yet ye have not, because ye ask not. Ye ask, and receive not, because ye ask amiss, that ye may consume it upon your lusts* (James 4:2-3).

God Can Heal It All

You need to understand that it is just as easy for God to heal the other diseases and sicknesses as it is for Him to heal the cancer. But if those other things are not bothering you, then they'll stay inside your body. Whatever matters most to you, particularly whatever causes you to seek God's help, matters most to God. If getting totally healed is your objective and is what is on your mind, then that is exactly what you will receive from God.

One Sunday evening a woman came into my healing line and said to me, "I have cancer in the lower part of my stomach, and my eyes are also bad. But I am not worried about my eyes, only about getting my cancer healed." I prayed for the cancer and God healed it. I already knew when she walked away that she had not received healing in her eyes. She did not ask for it. She neither expected nor believed that she would receive healing for her eyes. A few months later she will be awakened to the reality that her eyes need healing pretty badly. Then she will be asking God to heal her eyes next.

You'll receive healing when you realize you don't have to earn it.

Many people often seek for the baptism in the Holy Ghost for three months, six months, a year, three years, or even longer than that. Prior to receiving the baptism, they wonder what is keeping them from receiving it. With all their hearts, they really love God. They are walking in godly obedience. But then the enemy starts to play with their minds and makes them think that something is wrong with them or their lifestyle since they haven't receive the baptism. When they finally realize that the baptism in the Holy Spirit is not something they have to work for, but rather receive for the asking, they quickly receive it. Only then does it dawn on them that they've wasted a lot of time trying to earn it and merit it, when really it was far easier to just open up and receive than they thought.

You can apply the same train of thought to divine healing. Instead of trying to work for your healing, simply realize that your healing is a gift from God that is as easy as knowing one, two, and three. When you finally receive your healing and begin walking in it, you too will discover that you could have had your healing a long time before if only you had acted in faith and received what already belonged to you.

Although healing services create the environment that makes healing come more effortlessly, you don't have to wait for the crusade or service to come to town. You can receive your healing right now. Your healing comes through the knowledge of God's Word. Often healing services and crusade help to communicate that knowledge to you, making healing possible.

While I was in a Philadelphia, Pennsylvania, crusade, I was led to grab a man's crutches and break them into two pieces. He realized that my act of faith was an act of God. Instinctively he realized that his healing was present. He started shouting, praising, and magnifying God because he knew that he was healed. Each night thereafter, I had to tell the man to stay in his seat because he was so overwhelmed by what the Lord had done for him. He became so enthusiastic about his healing that he wanted to see others receive the same healing that he was enjoying. So he proceeded to break other people's crutches so they could receive their healing.

He thought that it would work for them since it worked for him. What he did not know was that it does not work for everyone. It is available to everyone, but only those who believe for it receive it. He could have broken everyone's crutches in the auditorium. But until they believed that healing was for them and that they would receive their healing that night on the spot, it would never happen.

There is no need for you to start feeling your way around the room without your glasses if you haven't released your faith for your eyes to be healed. We are not Christian Science. We are not telling you to deny any sickness or disease. We are simply informing you that Jesus can heal you no matter what ails you.

Get the Substance

Now faith is the substance of things hoped for, the evidence of things not seen (Hebrews 11:1).

You may get the substance yet not receive the evidence. However, God will give you so much of the substance that you won't have to worry about the evidence. You'll have enough substance to sustain you until the evidence arrives. When you actually look around, pretty much everything that you see is, in some way or another, substance. Your clothes, your hair, your house and furniture, even all kinds of books on faith are all substance. It's the same with faith; it's substance.

Many people live in a realm where they believe faith is super-mystical. They believe that when they get sick they have to mystically think themselves into wellness.

Unfortunately, they'll think themselves into a pretty severe headache and still won't be well. You can't use your mind to obtain godly promises, only your faith. Knowing that alone is the fundamental basis for faith. When you get the substance, you don't have to *try* to believe. It's already there.

It's the same way as when you got saved. You did not try to logically convince yourself that you were saved. You did not go around continuously repeating, "I know that I am saved. I've just got to believe that I am saved." No, not at all. Something deep down inside you knew that you were saved. That was the substance of your salvation. You knew that the old things were gone and now you were a brand-new person.

Therefore if any man be in Christ, he is a new creature: old things are passed away; behold, all things are become new (2 Corinthians 5:17).

When you go to church, you never say, "I hope the bench holds me up. It sure looks like it will. Do you suppose that the pastor came and took all the screws out from the bench when we were not here? I'd better sit down on it to check it first, to make sure that it will hold me up." That sounds silly, doesn't it? You just go ahead and sit down on the bench without even thinking twice about it. Yet, that silly conversation is the way most people treat God. They say, "I believe the promises of God are true. I've read the Word, and I hope that today is my day. I sure hope so. I am going to stand on God's promises and hope that they hold me up. I really wonder if all 42,000 promises of God are really sure, or if God is just talking."

When you think like that, after a while it becomes far more than a trivial thought. It becomes a heart issue. And when it becomes a heart issue, it becomes the main reason for why you cannot receive your healing from God, either in part or in full.

Healing starts in your heart, not your head.

Healing is not an issue of the head. It starts in your heart. When God heals you of a particular sickness, begin to praise Him for your healing right away. It doesn't matter what the symptoms are that still persist or how you are feeling in your body right then and there. All that matters is what God's Word said. What matters is that you know that you have been healed by God's power through His Word. That is your substance. Once you have grabbed hold of that reality, then you'll always have the healing that you desperately need. Ask, ask for all of it—everything that you need from Him—know that it belongs to you, receive it, and praise God for your healing every day that you live. If He heals you in part, praise Him in whole and watch what happens to the rest of your ailing body. You will receive a total healing.

Pleasant words are as an honeycomb, sweet to the soul, and health to the bones (Proverbs 16:24).

Chapter Ten

God Turns Woman
From Stone to Flesh
Jackie Rhodes' Story

"**C**ongratulations, Fletcher! You are the daddy of twin baby girls," announced the doctor. Dr. Rogers gave the surprising news immediately after delivering us on Wednesday afternoon September 28, 1910, in Delight, Arkansas. My mother was somewhat disappointed over our arrival, although Papa was smiling from ear to ear. You see, my parents were preparing for and expecting a baby boy and baby girl, but to their surprise out came two girls instead. Based on my fortuitous beginnings, unanticipated occurrences—even tragedies—would seem to follow me throughout the rest of my life.

Being so unexpected, Dad did not have time to purchase the clothing we needed. He didn't even have

127

names for us. Although he did not have all the necessary supplies for us, he deeply loved us, and that love would eventually help him overcome those initial setbacks. Although Daddy did not have very much, he managed to buy us a Jack and Jill bed. Dad, a cashier at the local bank, would inform any and everyone who came through the bank's doors that he was the proud father of twin baby girls. Quite some time after our birth we were given the birth names Hazel and Helen, although everyone always called us Jack and Jill.

My parents Leila Bell and John Fletcher Holcomb were happily married in their hometown, Locksburg, Arkansas, August 16, 1903. They were both Christians and also active members in their Baptist church. Three years after they got married they moved to Delight. When I was seven months old, unexpected tragedy struck our family when we suddenly lost my father. Since I was only seven months old when my daddy died, I have no real recollections of him even though family members told me that I was the apple of his eye.

Although I don't remember him, Mother instilled in me that I must love and cherish his memory, even if those memories were only the few stories that she would periodically share with me. My father's unexpected death left my mother a widow, alone to raise four children without an income or any support from her family. His death took such a toll on Mother that she went into a total state of shock and ended up unconscious, unable to get out of bed for several days.

Once my mother awakened from her semi-comatose state, to her dismay she discovered that my aunts and uncles were dividing her children, assuming that she was no longer mentally and emotionally capable to properly rear them. My brother, Carl Eugene, was five at the time, and my sister Ida Fletcher was three years old. Realizing the possibility of her home being split up gave her the needed determination to fight for her family. Resolute that she would not allow anyone to take her children away from her, she immediately began fighting for her health.

During the early 1900's, women did not work conventional jobs and few worked outside of the home. Most women then did domestic work for affluent people within society. Some women, the educated ones, were schoolteachers. Mom did not fit in any of those categories but desperately needed work to support all of us. God graciously blessed her and gave her an idea to open a hat shop in her home. She converted her living room into a hat shop and began to make hats for a living. Things were going well. But just when her business seemed to be flourishing to meet our needs, fate dealt us another blow. We lost our milk cow, which meant our food supply was scarce.

One afternoon, during my first year in grade school, we heard gunshots go off. That was our signal that there was a fire somewhere. We were all shaken when we heard the announcement that "Mrs. Holcomb's house is burning up!" By the time we reached our home, it was almost all in ashes. It all started because of some defect in our chimney. Practically everything we had was destroyed. We lost our home, the hat shop, and all our personal belongings.

After the fire we were showered with clothes, furniture, and money. Mama was able to buy an old store building with the cash she received and opened up her hat shop on one side and our living quarters on the other. Though our home was simply furnished, it was comfortable and clean, which made us feel right at home. Since my mother was the only milliner in town, her business grew rapidly. Prices were high and sales were good, but at the end of World War I she was left with expensive hats and a deflation in prices at hand. She struggled to adjust to the change, which is common after a war.

God took care of us through it all.

I can remember the day the peace treaty was signed like it was yesterday. Everyone was so excited. Horns were blowing and bells were ringing and in all the excitement I swallowed a safety pin.

I have a vivid memory of Mama preparing us for bed and kneeling down beside us as we said our prayers. I recall waking up in the middle of the night often and seeing Mama's tired body hunched over the dressing table, trimming hats by lamplight. Mama told us that she had tucked us into bed many nights not knowing where our next meal would come from. Nevertheless, she was diligent and never gave up. "As ye are faithful, so I will be unto you." God took care of us through it all.

Mama loved flowers and would take us into the yard with her to show us the beauties of nature and how God made the flowers for us to adore. When we as children acted up in front of company, all Mama had to do was give us a look and it set us straight.

Growing Up

One year the State Fair was going on at Little Rock. I yearned to go to the fair. My fervent desire to go the fair pushed me to beg my big brother Carl Eugene to take Jill and me. Considering that my sister and I had never been to Little Rock, Carl Eugene graciously gave in to my plea. We were overwhelmed with joy while dressing for our first adventure into Little Rock. I remember Jill and I taking our little red pocketbooks to hold our change in.

On our trip Jill and I adored all the tall buildings and beautiful homes, feasting our eyes on both sides of the street. When we reached Little Rock, Carl Eugene let us out in front of a dime store while he went to park. He told us to wait right there until he got back. As soon as he was out of sight, I grabbed Jill by the hand and we ran off into the store. I was overwhelmed with the size of the store. We had never seen such a big store before. I didn't know they made stores that enormous. We strolled up and down the aisles in amazement. Considering that we had good home training, we knew not to touch a thing.

I wanted to buy something for Mama. Everything was so pretty. All I could think to get was some beautiful flowers. When we finally reached the flower counter, I was astonished at the magnitude of plants and bulbs. I wished I could buy Mama a little bit of every kind, but they were way too expensive. Still, I spent all of my money and some of Jill's money to buy bulbs for our mother.

When we reached the main floor, I began to wonder if Carl Eugene was ever coming back. Needless to say, he was wondering where we were. We finally found our way back to the front of the store and there stood Carl Eugene. He looked very angry. I wondered why because Jill and I had been having so much fun. He yelled, "Where in the world have you been?" I said, "We didn't leave the store." He asked what I had in my sack. By that time I had nearly squeezed it in two. I proudly said, "Some flowers for Mama." When he gave me that smirky grin, I knew he was not upset anymore.

Shortly after we left the store we arrived at the fair. I used the rest of Jill's money to buy us a balloon. By this time I was very hungry and realized I had already spent every dime, not only of my money, but of Jill's also. Everywhere I looked they seemed to be selling food. I was starving but didn't dare ask Carl Eugene for anything. Next thing I knew, he asked us if we were hungry and bought us food. Thank God. The food was delicious. That day was a day to remember. That was the most fun I have ever had in my entire life.

In school I always made good grades and did not have to study too hard. I made the honor roll often. I played baseball, and I would run the bases for my friends because I was such a fast runner. Throughout school I was actively engaged in sports. I enjoyed all types of sports. Later I joined the first basketball team and played for three years.

As children, to entertain ourselves we would have fights. Girls would fight against girls and boys against boys. We would fight until the loser gave up. I have even fought two at a time and hardly ever gave up.

One day at school my teacher gave us an assignment on addresses of different departments of the government to write to. The department assigned to me was the weather department. I signed my name as usual: Jack Holcomb. When the material arrived, it was addressed to Mr. Jack Holcomb. A boy in my class teased me, calling me "Mr. Jack Holcomb, the weather director." Out of anger I jumped on him and we fought. Unfortunately he was bigger than I and our fight did not settle the feud. Every time I ran into that boy he would tease me. He teased me the whole school year. I hated him for months. Due to the constant teasing, later on in my life I called myself Jackie, which is more of a girl's name.

I never traveled or so much as went on a vacation as a child or as an adult. I spent most of my single life in Delight. My mother never owned a car, being a widow with four children. I often watched my friends with envy with their daddies to love them and give them nickels and take them places.

Although Mama was not always able to attend Sunday school and church because she was working, she made sure we attended every service. At age 12 I joined the Methodist church. That morning I stood at the altar before the minister and gave my heart to God. I was so touched that tears flowed from my eyes like a waterfall.

Growing up in the church, the vows I took that Sunday morning became a part of me. As a Christian I kept busy serving any way I could in church. I was involved in many church activities such as the junior league and the young people's organization, and I was the pianist for several years. At one time I was the secretary and treasurer of our Sunday school. I also taught Sunday school on several occasions. At age 16 I desired to become a foreign missionary but decided that receiving my high school education was much more important.

I prayed for God to bless us with a beautiful home with running water in the kitchen.

My favorite uncle was a wealthy salesman. He came to Delight once a month and made sure he'd stop by to visit us. On one of his trips to visit he insisted that I spend the weekend with him and his wife. I was overjoyed with excitement when Mama said yes. Their home was so beautiful with all the modern conveniences that we did not have. But what impressed me most was the running water in the kitchen. All you had to do was turn a little gadget and out flowed lots and lots of water. One day while at my uncle's home I went into the kitchen and turned on the water just to watch it run. My aunt came to the door and I quickly turned it off. We looked at each other with an unspoken silence, reading each other's mind.

Running water was a luxury to me, considering that we lived in a store and had to carry our water in gallon buckets from a public overflowing well. There was no water works in Delight at that time. That night I prayed for God to bless us with a beautiful home with running water in the kitchen. I was not able to sleep; I spent most of the night crying because Mama did not have all those nice things. When I got home, I was more appreciative to my mother.

Each fall my brother and sisters and I would pick cotton to help Mama buy our school clothes. We would race each other and I was often the champion picker for the day. One boy said the only reason I beat him was because I would talk a lot and as he stopped to listen I was able to keep "picking and talking." We were taught to work and did not mind it at all.

Oranges were a treat for us because we would only eat them at Christmas time. One Christmas Mama bought a whole box of oranges so we would have plenty. Carl Eugene snuck in and out of the kitchen eating oranges all day. Late that evening he felt very sick. Mama called the doctor and he quickly announced it must be appendicitis, but within a few hours his bowels were moved and he was fine.

My mother always dressed Jill and I alike although we are not identical twins. I always thought Jill was the pretty one. However, my oldest sister was the smartest in school. She would do her schoolwork and Carl Eugene would go behind her back and copy her work. She was also great at memorizing things. I remember on one occasion the children were out playing church and my sister was called on to pray. She prayed a long, interesting, educated prayer.

After they were done playing, one of the older children asked her where she learned to pray like that. My sister responded, "It's the one our professor says every morning in chapel."

Marriage and Home

I graduated from high school at age 17. I longed to go to college but that was impossible, especially since Carl Eugene had to quit school several years before to help Mama make a living so we girls could have an education. Mama's hat shop was put out of business by tailor-made hats. Tailor-made hats were the new trend and were sold in the dry good stores. I worked twice as hard in school so I could finish a year early. To accomplish my goal one summer I attended a six-week course. After all my hard work and diligence I was unable to find a job, which made me very upset. But then I was awarded a scholarship to take a business course. I went to school day and night and completed the course in three months. I accepted a job offer away from home, but I was never able to abandon Delight for good.

I met the love of my life, Joe Shelton Rhodes, while living in Delight, Arkansas. We were happily married on January 9, 1930. Reverend Mathis from the Smackover Baptist Church married us. Shortly after we were married, we moved into our first home in Camden. At the time my husband was working on the highways and I was working in an office.

The following December my only brother Carl Eugene was killed in a fatal car accident. My family and I felt like we could not go on without him. He was not only my one and only brother, but he had become a daddy to my sisters and I. My sister who was living and working out of town moved back home with Mama to help her run Carl Eugene's store. My family and I have been blessed to have the store up and running till this day.

One of the best days of my life was the day I gave birth to my son.

July 30, 1932, was one of the best days of my life— the day I gave birth to my son. Sonny was my pride and joy. We often called Sonny "The Depression Baby." Living during the depression is one of my most memorable hardships. Along with many others, I am blessed to be one of the survivors of the Great Depression.

The following year the unthinkable happened. My twin sister Jill was snatched out of my life. Jill and I had created a bond that could not be broken. I once felt as if our family was like a three-stranded cord, not easily broken. Now our family was being ripped apart by death.

Shelton never kept a steady job. So we moved around almost as often as the wind blew. We moved from state to state, Arkansas, Louisiana, and Texas, but Delight was always our refuge. We bought our home in Delight where I still reside today.

Sonny was the drive that I needed to move forward in my life. He was my comfort in many a dark and troubled hour when my burdens seemed too heavy to bear. I raised Sonny in the Methodist church. I remember one

Sunday when Sonny was very young, as we were entering church, I said, "Sonny, be a good boy because this is God's house." He looked up at me with a puzzled look and said, "Mother Jack, why you always say this is God's house? I not see God anywhere." It was at that moment that I realized it was time to explain to him what being a Christian was all about. I tried to instill in him high standards and the principles of Christian living. All I knew was to teach him what was taught to me. Thank God for my mother who helped develop me into who I am today.

One night I took Sonny to a donkey ball game. The crowd gathered as the players were introduced over the loudspeaker and everyone was overwhelmed with excitement. The game was sold out, so people were standing along the fence. Behind us was an old goat shed. Someone suggested that we climb up on it so we could get a better view of the game and sit down rather than stand. Shortly after we all made ourselves comfortable on the shed, it came tumbling down and we ended up piled on top of each other. When I came to, Sonny and others were gathered around trying to help me up. I was rushed to the hospital that night, but had a quick recovery.

When I woke up from my misery, we laughed and laughed at how we were all so excited about the game and did not pay any attention to the fact that we were all trying to force that flimsy goat shed to carry our weight. Most all of us were left with minor bruises and cuts. Since that accident I have had no desire to see another donkey ball game.

One Sunday Joe and I and two other couples decided to go fishing. I dressed Sonny for Sunday school to go to church with my mother that morning. While fishing I was standing on a slick log that extended out into the river. I slipped off of the log and nearly drowned. Although I never learned to swim, my survival instinct kicked in and I somehow managed to make it to the bank. I began kicking my feet and I shouted, "I'm swimming, I'm swimming!" The water was way over my head. Mama tried to put the guilt trip on me by saying the reason I fell was because I went fishing on a Sunday. She said it was a warning. I laughed at Mama, but her remark made me think twice about fishing on a Sunday. As a matter of fact, I never went fishing on a Sunday ever again.

As I look back on the year 1950, it was a year full of strife. I attended my mother's funeral on January 12. Sonny graduated from high school. Although Sonny's graduation was a great accomplishment, it became very stressful for me. Shortly after Sonny's graduation Joe and I were constantly at each other's throat. I took Sonny and we moved in with my sister. After that transition our lives were never the same. In September Joe and I got a divorce. Sonny also attended college that September. After attending college for one semester, Sonny dropped out and decided to join the Navy so he would not have to worry about being recruited by the Army. Considering that my health was failing and I was unable to go to work, Sonny felt obligated to take care of me.

Sick Unto Death

I fell very ill and my sickness lasted for two years. My doctor diagnosed me as having rheumatism since I had all the symptoms. I became very sore and stiff in my joints. As my joints would enlarge, they became very tender. I went to the most prominent doctors in Arkansas, but they could not help me. I endured all types of tests and still received no answer. The disease seemed to be tearing through my body rapidly.

My skin stuck to my bones.

My doctor suggested that I go to Mayo's. He made flight reservations for me to go. After examining me for four days, they called my sister Ida out into the hall and told her, "We cannot help your sister. You can take Jackie home at any time." Twenty-five skin specialists were called in, and unfortunately, not one of them could offer me a cure. I could not escape the harsh reality of my sickness.

Mayo diagnosed me with "scleroderma," which is the tightening of the derma skin to the bone, checking all circulation where it sticks. They gave me therapy light treatment followed by a cocoa butter massage. Though I received treatment twice a day, my skin would become so dry between treatments that it would be scaly and itch horribly. I also received shot treatments. Nonetheless, the disease was killing me slowly. As the swelling in my feet and hands would reduce, the derma would stick; as it stuck, my skin would itch and turn dark. My skin stuck so tight to my bones that my blood was not flowing properly. My body could not tell the difference between hot and cold. Parts of my body were dead. My nurse would often tiptoe to my bed to make sure I was still breathing.

My disease affected my appetite; I was unable to eat at times. I had to take gas medication before and after I attempted to eat. I often had gas attacks and was not able to pass the gas, which caused me to lose my breath when they laid me down. I became exhausted and weak after every attack. My illness disfigured my face, and I could hardly even open my mouth for food or drink. All I could eat was soft foods and drink liquids. My hair on my head and my eyebrows began falling out.

As the disease progressed, I could not stand the touch of clothing or bed sheets. One time I lay in bed for five months with a man's vest on. I could only lie on a feather bed. I would keep pillows under my knees and arms for comfort. I could not open or close my hands or even hold my head up. I was unable to stand tall; when I did stand, I was in hunched position and could only stand with assistance. Once I was helped up, but in order for me to sit back down I had to be pushed down by my shoulders.

My throat was closing in on me. My family and I knew the disease was in its last stage. My body was turning black all over. I began to lose pounds along with my mind; I could not think or talk clearly. I lost so much weight until I weighed barely 85 pounds. My body did not respond to any treatment. My doctor told my family and friends that I only had a few days left to live.

When I had arrived home from Mayo's, the doctor told me it was not necessary for me to stay in the hospital. I was basically sent home to die. My doctor sent me a registered nurse to continue my treatment and give me my shots every day.

Sonny was soon to come home from his boot training in the Navy while I was away at the Mayo's. Not knowing how long I was going to stay there, Sonny had a difficult time deciding whether to come home or come visit me in the hospital. Fortunately, before his discharge I was sent home. Upon leaving the Mayo's and going to the airport, my flight was canceled due to the horrid weather. We were stuck in the Mayo's for four additional days due to a dreadful snowstorm. We were put up in a hotel directly across from the hospital. All we wanted to do was go home, but day after day we were disappointed until finally, on the fourth day, the storm went its separate way.

Before we hopped on the plane, we called Sonny with the great news that we were on our way home so he could meet us in Delight. Sonny arrived in Delight a few days later. He was very worried and melancholy about me being so sick that I had to stay in bed. Sonny carried me to the car each day and lay me on a bed made in the back seat of his car just for me so that I could receive my Mayo treatments. We all hated to see Sonny go ten days later back to the Navy base. After Sonny left, the disease began to overtake my body. I was only getting worse as the days went by.

My sister Ida suggested that we tell Sonny the truth about how horrible my sickness had become. She was afraid that I would die any day and the shock would be too much for Sonny to handle. So Ida decided to write him a letter saying that she believed it was possible that I might not live much longer.

My doctors told Ida that the treatments were not working. After Sonny read the letter he consulted his commanding officer. His commanding officer looked up at him and said, "Rhodes, if that was my mother, I'd get out of here and go stay with her as long as she lived." Sonny said, "That's what I'd like to do." He said, "If you will do what I tell you, you will be out of here and with her in two weeks." Sis got him an emergency leave and he came home.

While he was home he contacted whomever he needed to say he could get as much time off as possible. Before I could blink an eye, he was home with a Hardship Discharge. I was overwhelmed with satisfaction that he was home. I begged him to stay near me all the time. Often times Sonny would sit and talk to me and then get up and walk from room to room. He informed me after I was healed that he left my room because he could not stand to see me that sick and he just knew I was going to die. When I was healed Sonny had been home two weeks to the exact day.

My Divine Healing

Next thing I knew, I heard of the Jack Coe meeting. God sent one of His servants to my bedroom to tell me that Jesus still heals. Though I had never been to a divine healing service before, my family was hopeful of anything that would save me from dying. Sonny became interested and began to study and meditate on the Holy Scriptures, which led him to Brother Jack Coe's meeting. This was all so new to him that he was astonished to see the power of God move in that place. Blind eyes were opened, deaf ears could hear, crippled people were throwing away their crutches and shouting the victory. I said, "Well, Sonny, what do you think about it for me?" He said, "All you have to have is faith." I asked him if he had the faith and he said, "I don't know, Mother, but you have."

I cried out to the Lord in prayer, asking Him for a clear mind and faith to heal my body. On the third day my mind was clear and I was able to discuss going to Jack Coe's meeting with my family. My family had doubts because we lived a hundred miles away from Little Rock and they were afraid that I might die on the way. Ida discussed our plan with our pastor and he told her to take me to the meeting because there was no limit to the power of God. Knowing in our hearts that this was our only hope and after receiving my pastor's blessing, Sonny, Ida, and I loaded into the car and headed to the meeting. They made a bed for me in the backseat of the car so I could be as comfortable as possible.

Since I was unable to walk, Sonny carried me into the tent meeting and laid me on a stretcher during the service that night. As I lay in that stretcher amazed by God's healing power, I thought to myself, *Can God heal me too?* Within seconds it was as if God was answering me. Brother Jack Coe came over to me and said, "Do you believe that Jesus can heal you?" I said, "Yes." He commanded, "In the name of Jesus, sit up." I pushed the sheet back with my feet and sat up all by myself for the first time in years. As I sat there, Brother Coe prayed for me. I don't remember all that he said, but I specifically remember him anointing me and saying, "Lord, heal this woman from the top of her head to the sole of her feet."

I felt the healing virtue flow through my whole body and I instantly knew I was healed. Evangelist Coe looked down at me and said, "Do you believe you are healed?" I answered yes. He then said, "In the name of Jesus, get up and walk." I did, and I have been walking ever since. As I stood I could feel the presence of my sister's hands as she reached forward to help me stand. Evangelist Coe said, "Don't touch her; she won't fall." I did not fall, either. When I walked back to my bed, they started to put me on it and Evangelist Coe said, "Don't put her back to bed; we just got her up." Someone gave me a chair and as I sat, Evangelist Coe started talking to me. He said, "You are healed; go home and eat." Those words rung in my ears for several days because my appetite was gone, my throat was almost completely closed, and my organs would not function. But as I could hear Evangelist Coe's kind voice, and knowing that he was a servant of God, I knew I must try and try hard.

"In the name of Jesus, get up and walk."

On my way back home I was able to sit in the front seat. We arrived home at about 2 o'clock on Sunday morning and I was able to attend Sunday school and church. My pastor and my church family were surprised to see me, but they rejoiced with me because they knew it was the work of the Lord. After church my Sunday school teacher told me she felt like she was facing someone who had been raised from the dead. Before I was healed I was very thin and my skin was black. The first seven weeks after I was healed, I went to church every night testifying to my healing. Although I was born and raised in the Methodist church, I enjoy going to all churches to tell them of the great blessing I have received.

When Evangelist Coe prayed for me, the disease instantly left my body. In Matthew 9:29 it says, *"According to your faith be it unto you."* So it was with me. As I grew in faith, I also grew in health. The third day after my healing there was great progress; I could open my mouth and swallow with no complication. I also could move my stiff ankle and straighten out my legs. I was even able to comb my hair again.

I have been healed for three years now and I am enjoying the simple pleasures of life that I once missed out on due to my sickness. I weigh 111 pounds, which is more than I ever weighed in my life. I have gained 26 pounds. I have my appetite back. I have no pains whatsoever. My skin is back to its normal color; I can take baths and I can perspire again.

I am enjoying life. I can drive, play the piano, sew, cook, wash, iron, mop, and sweep just to name a few things. I am so thankful for my healing, and I always enjoy telling others what the Lord has done for me. I accept any opportunity to testify for Him. I hope to encourage others and tell them that the same God who healed me can heal them. Not only did He give me life, He also gave me a new life—one worth living.

Life for Me Today

Before the summer of 1951, the possibility of asking the living Lord a direct question and receiving a specific answer had never once crossed my mind. Finding myself in an unexpected crisis is what pushed me to take a leap of faith. It was like giving God a blank check of my life and trusting that He would fill my every void. The moment I surrendered my life to the Lord, I felt His Spirit governing my life. I learned that God wants us to live life in divine health and abundant wealth, which ultimately will bring us happiness also.

It has been three amazing years since I have been healed. I am enjoying my life to the fullest. It's hard for me to believe that at one time I actually thought my life was coming to an end. The Lord has shown me that He puts people in your life to bless you. The one that God blessed me with is my sister Ida. We are living and enjoying life together. She has been such an inspiration to me. There were no limits to what she would do for me. Many days she would be so tired and worn out after working all day at the store and caring for me in her spare time, but to me she looked like an angel.

Often Ida has said that for her labor the Lord has given her double. I have never known anyone to be so diligent in all her efforts. She never once disagreed to anything that might add to my comfort or pleasure. I am fortunate to have a sister so unselfish and considerate. Our home is a place of peace. We own our own grocery store. We are blessed with many Christian friends whose prayers have strengthened us in our time of need.

My only son Sonny was married on February 1, 1953, to Alice Blackmon of Glenwood, Arkansas, in the Methodist church in Delight, Arkansas. Though I was so excited for Sonny, I could not help but shed a few tears in all the excitement. Watching them kneel at the altar vowing to love each other till death do they part, so young, so sweet, and so happy, I felt that I did not lose my son but gained a daughter. The Lord has given their union His richest blessings.

Words can never express what the Lord has done for me. The Lord has blessed me to be a blessing to those who are on their beds of affliction and to convert non-believers. My mission, God's mission, is to let people know that God is the only One who can heal their bodies and save their souls from the pit of destruction. Because the Lord has healed me through prayer, I have become a prayer intercessor, praying for anyone who walks across my path.

My sister Ida and I recently returned from Evangelist Jack Coe's 4th of July revival in Dallas, Texas. It is always wonderful to be in the presence of souls being saved, the sick being healed, and people being baptized with the Holy Spirit. Ida and I were both water baptized at the revival. Shortly after our baptism, my sister received the Holy Ghost. We had an awesome time feasting upon the blessings of the Lord. The Lord does what we allow Him to do because He is the same living God yesterday, today, and forever.

Afterthoughts

※══ ══※

In these pages of *Curing the Incurable* we are explaining how to receive your healing. Jesus Christ is the Healer and He delights in curing the seemingly incurable. If you are in any situation where you need a touch from God, know that He can change you, even right now. "All things" really are possible for those who are in Christ Jesus. It is one thing to know that God can heal, but it is a totally different thing to know *why* He will heal you. When you recognize why He is obligated to heal you, you will walk in your promise so much sooner.

We live in a world where tragedy, sickness, and disease have become far too commonplace. This has left so many people feeling totally hopeless. Thanks be to God that we have a blessed hope in Christ Jesus. He has given us the step-by-step process in His Word on how we can receive our healing. It does not matter what kind of disease or sickness you suffer from; God can heal you. Cancer, tuberculosis, lymphoma, kidney failure, blindness, heart disease, asthma—all are on the same level with God. They are all sicknesses that if left alone can prove fatal to the human body.

God has a burning desire that each and every one of His creation be whole and complete. That desire led Him to give His only Son as a sacrifice, making it possible for us to receive healing over and over again. Therefore, whether or not one receives his or her healing is largely based on his or her faith in Christ and His Word.

God is a sovereign God; therefore, He does what He wants and when He wants to do it. This explains why some are healed and others are not. Though He is sovereign, we cannot discount who God is. It is His nature to heal, set free, and deliver no matter what. But, on the other hand, there are some things we can do through faith to activate God's healing power, and there are some things we have no control over.

There are many ways you can be healed. Some sicknesses can only be cured through prayer and fasting. Others are cast out by the laying on of hands. Some are cast out in foolish ways. The Word says God uses the foolish things to confuse the wise. The bottom line is God is a Healer. It is His nature to heal the sick.

God's main purpose of calling His people to do His work is to save unbelievers from their sins. In becoming a believer, you must have faith to move mountains. You also must be humble. In addition, the Lord requires you to forgive those who have wronged you. In doing these things you can experience the wholeness of God.

There is nothing like having the peace that passes all understanding. We must find time to pray, read the Bible, and wait on the Lord. When you are in God's will for your life, you cannot go wrong. God desires to bless His people, so we need to be open to receive all that God has for us. He has a perfect plan for each and every one of our lives—if only we would discover it and walk in it every day of our lives.

If you are sick in your body, struggling with cancer, kidney failure, AIDS, sickle cell, asthma, or anything else, God can and desires to cure you. God is just waiting on you to exercise your faith and come to Him asking and knowing that He will heal your every disease. God is your provider, healer, lover; He is the I AM who is whoever and whatever you need Him to be. God meets you where you are in your time of need.

God desires for you to seek Him first, and all these things shall be added unto you. There is nothing like having a personal relationship with Christ. He wants you to love on Him, praise Him, and seek Him early in the morning when you get up. When you make God a priority, He will make you a priority. Though it may seem like you have to give so much of yourself to become saved, it is just the opposite. If you give your life to God, He then is able to help you mend the broken pieces in your life.

Knowing that Jesus is here to rid us of pain and sickness itself brings peace. Pain and sickness are by-products of sin. Christ died to forgive us of our sins so that we can live "the good life"—the life He originally intended for us to live. He loves each and every one of us as His child. As a good daddy desires for his child to have the best and be the best in life, so does our Father in heaven desire this for us.

The God we serve is an all-powerful God; He does things to get His point across however He may have to. This is the reason God heals in different stages. He heals some instantly. Others have to activate their faith in order to be healed. Then there are those who are healed gradually over time. In each instance God gets the glory, which He is worthy of.

In every miracle that God performs there is a lesson to be learned. That is why not everyone can be healed instantly, blessed financially, or given a miracle just because he or she asks. The Lord knows what you are going to do even before you do it. He foreknew you even before you were formed in your mother's womb. He knows what you can handle. He knows when you are ready to receive from Him. That's why everything is done in God's timing.

The Lord desires for us to get rid of doubt and disbelief. He wants us to open our hearts. He also wants us to get rid of fear. These are some of the things the enemy tries to use to keep us from receiving our healing from Almighty God. He is not slack at what concerns His children. Often times we put limits on God without even knowing or realizing it.

We must praise God in our infirmities. When we are sick and diseased and beaten down by the things of this world, we must still praise Him. In all things give thanks. When God sees the spirit in us that will not quit or give up on God no matter what the circumstance, it moves Him to act. *"Weeping may endure for a night, but joy cometh in the morning"* (Psalm 30:5b).

It is God's desire that we may prosper and be in health. *"Beloved, I wish above all things that thou mayest prosper and be in health, even as thy soul prospereth"* (3 John 2). God created us for His glory. In order for us to glorify God in our bodies, we must be healthy and prosperous. He wants us to have the total package. Everything about God is excellent. Therefore we must strive for excellence also.

Understand that God does not make you sick. God cannot give you what is not in Him. I have heard many say, "Well, if it is God's will, I've got to die of something." It is never God's will for you to die of sickness and disease. He gave His Son Jesus so that we may have life. When we see people who are sick, often times they think God has abandoned them. That is not the case. Instead, they may have given up on God.

The Bible says that we men will do greater miracles than Jesus Christ did when He walked the earth (see John 14:12). This is a prime example of how much He desires for us to be healed. God never changes, but we do. He created us in His image and gave us dominion over the earth. Then Adam and Eve fell into sin and everything changed. Though we may change, *"Jesus Christ* [is] *the same yesterday, and to day, and for ever"* (Hebrews 13:8).

About the Author

J ack Coe was a well-known healing evangelist and tent revivalist during the 1940's and 50's. He gave his life to the Lord while a young man dying of alcoholism. Later he received the baptism of the Holy Spirit at a revival meeting. While in the Army during World War II, Jack Coe learned to follow God and preach to his fellow soldiers despite persecution and criticism—even to the point of getting locked up for being a "religious fanatic."

Jack Coe's boldness and fearlessness and whole-hearted devotion to God were characteristics of his tent revival ministry. He and his family traveled around the country holding crusades and meetings, sharing the good news of Jesus Christ and His power to heal.

In the early 1950's Jack Coe founded the Herald of Healing Children's Home in Dallas, Texas, for orphaned and unwanted children. He also started a Faith Home where seriously ill people could come, hear the Word, and stay until they received their healing. At that time Jack Coe also began radio broadcasting, and even made plans to televise the crusade meetings. In 1952 he and another pastor founded the Dallas Revival Center, which saw packed crowds at every service.

Jack and his wife Juanita had six children. The eldest, Jack Coe, Jr., still carries on today in the healing and revival ministry.

Photos

‡⁼‡

Tent outside from the air.

Inside the tent.

Church inside.

Inside the tent.

Jack Coe & wife by fireplace.

Jack Coe praying for a woman.

Jack Coe with healed woman.

Jackie Rhodes shortly after being prayed for by Jack Coe in 1951.

Jackie Rhodes one year later showing how her condition has improved.

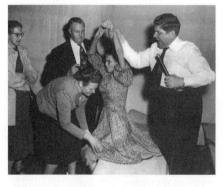

Jack Coe & wife praying for a woman's legs.

Jack Coe, Sr.